Beyond Conversion

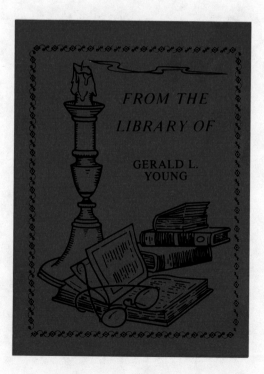

Beyond Conversion

Paul W. Powell

Broadman Press
Nashville, Tennessee

4252–60
ISBN: 0–8054–5260–5

Dewey Decimal Classification: 248
Subject heading: CHRISTIAN LIFE// SPIRITUAL LIFE

Library of Congress Catalog Card Number: 77-80942
Printed in the United States of America

To the men who have influenced me the most . . .

My father, Jodie Powell

My pastor, John M. Wright

My sons, Kent and Mike

My brothers, Ray Condra and Ronnie Wilson

My staff, Dennis Parrott, Bill Baker and Allan Cox

My friends, all the men in the churches I've served.

Preface

A Japanese master was once asked, "What is the most difficult part of a picture?" He answered, "The part that is to be left out."

That's the difficulty that I have had with this book. There is so much to the Christian life beyond conversion that it is hard to know what to leave out. J. B. Gambrell said, "Conversion is the end of the Christian life—but it's the front end." How right he is. But far too often we have won people to Christ, baptized them, and then left them to drip dry all alone. The great commission, the apostolic examples, and Christian concern demands that we take people in their Christian life beyond conversion to Christian maturity.

The Philippian jailer's famous question to Paul, "Sirs, what must I do to be saved?" was relatively easy to answer. One sentence was enough. However, Paul often wrote whole books to instruct people such as the jailer on how to conduct themselves in their new life.

The question, "What should I do now that I am saved?" is far more complex. And it merits a plain, biblical, and practical answer.

As I have written these pages I have tried to keep

foremost in my mind those questions, needs, dangers, and responsibilities facing the new convert. I offer these pages with a prayer that they will help Christians, new and old, go beyond conversion and on to maturity in their Christian experience.

Contents
Beyond Conversion There Is . . .

Beyond Conversion

1
Growing—On to Maturity

Recently a Christian friend shared her testimony in our church. She said she was converted when she was twelve years old. Years later, at the age of twenty-nine, a tragedy occurred in her life. Then she realized that at the age of twenty-nine she was still a twelve-year-old Christian. She had been born again seventeen years earlier but had failed to grow.

Retarded growth is tragic in any area of life. One of the most wonderful things in all the world is birth. It is a mystery that no one really understands. But while birth is a wonder, if there were to be no growth after birth we would worry. If we learned that one out of every two babies born this year would die before reaching maturity, we would become alarmed. We would call on our doctors, our health officials, and government agencies to do something about this terrible waste of life.

For people to be born and never to grow into maturity is a terrible waste. Yet something like that happens in spiritual life all the time. People are born again. They become a part of the family of God through faith in Jesus Christ. But they fail to go on from that initial experience of birth to maturity in the Christian life. What a tragic waste.

The writer of Hebrews was keenly aware of this and said: "Therefore leaving the principles of the doctrine of Christ, let us go on unto perfection; not laying again the foundation of repentance from dead works, and of faith toward God. Of the doctrine of baptisms, and of laying on of hands, and of resurrection of the dead, and of judgment. And this will we do, if God permit" (Heb. 6:1–3).

This passage of Scripture is a great challenge. God's people are urged to move from their initial Christian experience to maturity in their Christian lives.

These verses are written against the backdrop of scolding people for failing to grow. His readers had been Christians long enough to become teachers by this time. But they hadn't grown and they still needed to be taught by somebody else. By this time they should have been eating the strong meat of God's Word. But they weren't able to digest it spiritually. They were still bottle babies so far as the spirit was concerned. They had had the initial birth experience. They had been born into the kingdom of God. But there is more to the Christian life than birth. There is more to the Christian life than being saved. There is more to the Christian life than that initial experience. So we are challenged in Hebrews 6 to go on to perfection.

The word "perfection" in the Greek does not in any way imply sinlessness. It is best interpreted maturity. So we are being challenged to go on to maturity in the Christian life. This Greek word for perfection is used in many different ways in the Bible. Sometimes it is used to describe a man who is fully grown in contrast to a lad who is not yet developed physically. Sometimes it is used to describe a person who has mastered a subject in contrast to a person who is just a beginner. If something is perfect, it fulfills its intended purpose. It accomplishes what it was created to do. So we, as God's people, need to go on in our Christian experience to become what God wants us to become—to fulfill our intended purpose.

What is God's plan, or purpose, for your life and for mine? The apostle Paul tells us in no uncertain terms that the standard of Christian maturity is Jesus Christ himself. He says that God has given to the church "Apostles; and some prophets; and some evangelists; and some pastors and teachers; . . ." so that we may come eventually "Unto the measure of the stature of the fulness of Christ" (Eph. 4:11–13). So the goal of the Christian life is that we might become like Jesus Christ. The goal is to grow up to be like him.

We must never be content just to escape hell. Nor can we be content just to reach heaven. In the interim, we must grow into the fullness of the stature of Christ. We must become like our Savior. That's the challenge of this passage of Scripture. Paul is saying, "Let us go on to spiritual maturity. Let us go on to become all that God wants us to be. Let us go on in our Christian life until we become like Jesus Christ."

As he gives us this exhortation he suggests three things that are necessary if we are to reach Christian maturity.

Maturity Requires a Great Departure

Paul begins by saying, "Therefore, leaving the principles of the doctrine of Christ, let us go on." Before we
can ever reach maturity we must leave the ABC's of the
Christian faith. We must leave the foundational stones so
that we can go on in Christian growth. The word "leave"
does not mean to abandon or to forsake. It means leave
as a tree leaves its roots to rise up into the air. It is still
attached to the roots, it is still based upon the roots, but
it grows from the roots to become a tree. It means to
leave as a building leaves its foundations and goes on to
become a superstructure. It is still attached to the foundation, but it has gone on from that foundation to become a complete building.

The Christian life must have roots, but it cannot be all
roots. The Christian life must have foundations, but it
cannot all be foundations. So, having built our lives upon
the principles of the doctrine of Christ, we must then go
on to become everything that God wants us to be.

What are the foundational elements of the Christian
faith? Six of them are listed in this passage of Scripture.

1. Repentance from dead works. The Christian life
begins with repentance from dead works. Dead works
are the efforts to save ourselves by being good.

2. Faith. This is openhearted trust in God.

3. The doctrine of baptism. This is the outward and
ceremonial expression of our repentance and faith. Having turned from dead works and having turned in faith to
God, we are to be baptized as an outward and ceremonial expression of our commitment to him.

4. The laying on of hands. This has reference to receiving the Holy Spirit. The laying on of hands often preceded receiving the Holy Spirit in the first century.

5. The resurrection of the dead.

6. The judgment. This is the time when we shall stand before God and give an account of ourselves to him. These are the foundational stones of the Christian life. We build our lives upon them. But we don't settle down there. We go on from there to Christian maturity.

A careful look at these six foundational stones is revealing. The first two, repentance and faith, are the first steps in the Christian's life. The second two, baptism and the laying on of hands, are the external and ceremonial expressions of that initial experience. The last two, the resurrection and the judgment, have to do with the end of the Christian life. So the writer is saying this: we must not get so caught up on the front end of the Christian life or on the tail end of the Christian life that we forget the great in-between of growth and development.

Some churches spend all of their time talking about salvation. Others spend all of their time talking about the end of time. And they never go on to maturity. We must not fall victim to that. We must go on to become like Jesus Christ. We must move off the foundation and on to a higher level of Christian living.

Maturity Requires a Firm Determination

Next the writer says, "And this we will do." That is a statement of determination, of high resolve. We can't be content to remain infants in our Christian experience.

We must go on to Christian maturity. And that takes resolve. No one drifts into Christian maturity, but you can drift into sin. The Bible says, "Therefore, we ought to give the more earnest heed to the things which we have heard, lest at any time we should let them slip" (Heb. 2:1).

The word "slip" in the Greek means to drift. It describes the ship that has broken loose from the dock and has been taken by the current downstream and away from the harbor of safety. In exactly the same way, many people drift into sin. They don't intend to do it. Sometimes they aren't even aware it is happening, but they turn loose of Christ for a moment and begin to drift away from him. You can drift into sin. But you cannot drift into Christian maturity.

You can fall into sin. The Bible says, "Brethren, if a man be overtaken in a fault, ye which are spiritual, restore such an one in the spirit of meekness; considering thyself, lest thou also be tempted" (Gal. 6:1). The verb "overtake" in the Greek means to trip up and fall accidentally. It describes a man who is walking down an icy road when suddenly his feet slip out from under him and before he knows it he is on the ground. Quite often that happens to people spiritually. They accidentally fall into sin. But if you ever become mature in the faith, you will have to climb there. You reach it only by true determination.

In 1925 George Mallory and a group of Englishmen determined to climb Mt. Everest. Mt. Everest is the highest point on the face of the earth. It is 29,028 feet high. The party started climbing the mountain and set up a base camp at 25,000 feet. George Mallory and one of his companions continued the climb while the rest of the men stayed at the base camp below. The two men lost their footing and fell to their deaths. Today their bodies still lie somewhere near the top of Mt. Everest buried beneath the snow.

Later, one of the climbers was giving a lecture before a large audience in London. He told about the trials and the hardships of trying to climb Mt. Everest. He turned to a large slide of the mountain on the screen behind him. Then he said to the mountain, "Everest, we tried to conquer you once, and you overcame us. We tried to conquer you a second time, and you were too much for us. But, Everest, we will conquer you yet, for you can't grow and we can." It's that kind of determination that will enable you to reach the summit of Christian maturity. It will not happen accidentally. You cannot drift into it. You cannot fall into it. You've got to climb the mountain of Christian maturity with firm determination.

Maturity Requires a Godly Dedication

Having talked about the destination and determination, the writer now talks about dedication when he says he will go on to maturity "if God permits." It takes that kind of dependence to become mature. Our life depends upon God's strength, his power, and his help. Those who have lived godly lives have achieved Christian maturity. They have learned the secret of depending upon God for every need of life, even the ability to grow in Christian maturity.

The apostle Paul prefaced his desire to visit Corinth by saying, "If the Lord permit" (1 Cor. 16:7). James warns us about planning our future without taking God into account when he says: "Go to now, ye that say, To day or to morrow we will go into such a city, and continue there a year, and buy and sell, and get gain: Whereas ye know not what shall be on the morrow. For what is your life? It is even a vapour, that appeareth for a little time, and then vanisheth away. For that ye ought to say, If the Lord will, we shall live, and do this, or that" (Jas. 4:13–15).

All of life is lived in dependence upon God. We need to move on to Christian maturity, and we can if God strengthens and helps us. None of us need to wonder about the goal of our life. We are to become like Jesus Christ.

But it takes a departure. It takes determination. It takes dependence if we are ever going to reach that goal. And it is my hope and prayer that you will come to this place of high resolve. You must go beyond conversion if you are to complete maturity in the Christian faith.

2
Praying—Developing a Strong Prayer Life

Two spiritual practices are indispensable in reaching Christian maturity. The first is prayer. The second is Bible study. These are like the two wings of a giant bird. If you keep both of them going, you can soar to spiritual heights. If you stop using either, you will plunge to spiritual destruction. In this chapter we will discuss building a prayer life. In the next chapter we will deal with studying the Bible.

The single most important factor in growing to Christian maturity is prayer. Its importance cannot be overestimated. It is the difference in Christianity being a form and a force. Every great servant of God has been a man of prayer.

The Christian life is a life of dependence. It is not an "Operation Bootstrap." It is not a matter of believing in Jesus and doing the best you can. It is not joining the church and getting a do-it-yourself kit. It is living in constant fellowship with and dependence upon God. Through him there is strength and help and victory. Prayer is your connection with God.

The importance of prayer can best be seen in the life of Jesus. Jesus on his knees is the greatest argument there

is for prayer. As someone has said, "God had only one
son who lived without sin. But he has had no sons who
have lived without prayer." Jesus was constantly in
prayer. He prayed before he ate, before great decisions,
and in the garden of Gethsemane. Sometimes he prayed
all night long. His was the most beautiful life ever lived.
And it was punctuated with prayer.

The disciples were so impressed with the prayer life of
Jesus that they asked him, "Lord, teach us to pray"
(Luke 11:1). They had heard him preach eloquent sermons, but they never asked, "Lord, teach us to preach."
They saw him perform amazing miracles but they never
said, "Lord, teach us to work miracles." They recognized
that the secret of his great life was in his communion
with God through prayer. That's why they said, "Lord,
teach us to pray."

In response to their request Jesus gave them and us
the Lord's Prayer (Matt. 6:5–17). In addition to the
Lord's Prayer Jesus taught many other things about
prayer. He said, "Ask, and it shall be given you; seek,
and ye shall find; knock, and it shall be opened unto you:
For every one that asketh receiveth; and he that seeketh
findeth; and to him that knocketh it shall be opened"
(Matt. 7:7–8).

On another occasion he said, "Men ought always to
pray, and not to faint" (Luke 18:1). The word "ought"
implies a moral obligation. Prayer is not only a privilege,
it is also a duty, or a responsibility. Jesus said that men
ought to pray because he knows what prayer can do. It
can revive a church. It can empower a preacher. It can

save a soul. It can strengthen a life. And because prayer
has such great power, men have a moral obligation to
pray. The alternative to praying is to faint. It is to fall out
and melt away in the difficult task of living. Prayer then
is the source of strength that enables us to stand up to
life.

The disciples, having watched and listened to Jesus,
also became men of prayer. They discovered that prayer
is God's way for us to obtain his blessings (Phil. 4:6; John
16:23). They discovered that prayer is the way to find
personal fellowship (1 John 1:3). They discovered that it
is the source of power to overcome temptation (Eph.
6:18). And they discovered that prayer is an aid in witnessing (Rom. 10:1).

Prayer is a power, but it is not a substitute for work. It
is not a substitute for plowing a field, seeing a doctor, or
studying for a test. It is not a substitute; it is a supple-
ment. It is a request that God will do more for us than we
can do for ourselves. It is a request for a miracle. When
my child is sick, I don't just pray, or just take him to a
doctor. I do both. I want what antibiotics can do, but I
also want what God can do.

Prayer then grows out of the conviction that God is my
father and that he stands ready, willing, and able to help
me in all of the circumstances of life. One of the
tragedies of most modern disciples is that they are trying
to live without prayer. That's why we are weak and
anemic in our spiritual lives. We have neglected communion with God. Many teachers stroll into their Sunday School classes with quarters in one hand and quar-

terlies in the other and wonder why they cannot hold the attention of the class. Many choirs sing with artistic skill, but no one is stirred by their music. Many a preacher buys a book of sermons and gets his message from it rather than from the Bible, and no one is saved. We are relying upon human ability rather than divine resources. We cannot have God's power in our lives unless we pray.

So, developing a strong prayer life is essential to a victorious Christian life. The essential ingredients of an effective prayer life are seen clearly in the life of Daniel. Daniel is one of the great men of the Old Testament. He lived a beautiful and exemplary life. He was taken into captivity by Nebuchadnezzar, the king of Babylon, when he conquered Jerusalem. Because of his intelligence and promise he was taken to the king's court and trained for diplomatic service. God blessed his good life and humble spirit and he rose to prominence and favor. He soon became a victim of jealousy by other men in the kingdom.

They observed his life for a period of time. They realized that if they were going to discredit Daniel it would have to be at the point of his religion. They could not get him on any other issue. So they persuaded the king to pass a decree to put to death anyone who prayed to any god except the king. Daniel heard about the decree but he was not deterred by it. He had been a faithful follower of Jehovah all of his life and the decree of the king was not going to change that. So, the Bible says, "Now when Daniel knew that the writing was signed, he went into his house; and his windows being open in his chamber toward Jerusalem, he kneeled upon his knees three times a day, and prayed, and gave thanks before his God, as he did aforetime" (Dan. 6:10).

In this brief excerpt from the life of Daniel, we see the essential ingredients of a strong prayer life. If you want to build an effective prayer life, you need to follow the practices of Daniel. His life teaches us five things about building an effective prayer life.

We Must Establish the Habit of Prayer

When Daniel heard the decree of the king, the Scriptures say that he went to pray "as he did aforetime." Daniel's prayer life was not just an emergency measure. It was not something that he did when problems greater than he could handle arose. Prayer was a long-established habit of his life. And so he was simply doing what he had been doing all along. Prayer was his way of dealing with life.

A crucial question for every believer is this: How will I handle life and its problems? The Christian's motto ought to be: "Life is precious; handle it with prayer." Our first inclination ought to be to pray. Our life is not to be lived at the mercy of moods, pressures, or crises. It is to be lived in complete dependence upon God. So we too should make prayer the habit of our lives.

I cannot overestimate the importance of good spiritual habits in your life. We are all creatures of habit, so we need to establish some good ones. When we think about habits, we usually think of bad ones that we need to break. However, there are some good habits that we need to establish. Every great servant of God including Jesus has had them. The Scriptures say concerning Jesus, "And, as his custom was, he went into the synagogue on the sabbath day" (Luke 4:16). Going to the synagogue was a habit in the life of Jesus.

What are the spiritual habits of your life? Do you know what it is to have a time and a place of prayer like Daniel? Martin Luther said, "Prayer is a powerful thing, for God has linked himself thereto." Alfred Lord Tennyson said, "More things are wrought by prayer than this world dreams of." You can do more than pray after you have prayed, but you can't do more than pray until after you have prayed. If prayer is not the habit of your life, then I urge you to begin now. It is the key to spiritual growth.

You Need to Find a Place for Prayer

Daniel also had a place for praying. The Scriptures tell us that it was in his apartment, by the window, facing Jerusalem. Jerusalem was the city of God. It was there that the house of God was located. Jerusalem and the Temple in a very special way represented the presence of God. No doubt Daniel found great comfort and strength in looking toward Jerusalem as he offered his prayers to God. This was his place of prayer.

Prayer can never be relegated to just one place. Jonah prayed from the belly of the big fish. Peter prayed from a rooftop. Hezekiah prayed from a bed of affliction. Hagar prayed while in the wilderness. Jairus prayed on the street. Paul prayed while he was in jail. Jesus prayed

while on the mountaintop. The thief prayed from the
cross. And you can pray anywhere, anytime. Some
people pray while they are driving down the street.
Some pray while they are washing dishes. Some pray
while they are shaving. Any place a Christian finds himself can be a place of prayer.

However, it will help our prayer life if we have a
definite place where we meet God on a regular basis.
The closest Jesus ever came to telling us where to pray
was when he told us to enter into our closet for prayer
(Matt. 6:6). When Jesus talked about entering into our
closet to pray, he was not emphasizing the location of
prayer. He was instead stressing the importance of attitude and atmosphere of prayer. Prayer is never to be
for display, but for communion with God. The advantage
of entering into a quiet place is that it shuts out the
distractions of the world.

One of the major problems most of us face in our
prayer life is the problem of distractions and a wandering
mind. There are many things you can do to help solve
this problem. For one thing, you can pray out loud. This
helps your concentration. Use a prayer list. This keeps
your mind on the track. Keep a notepad and pencil
handy. Then when extraneous ideas or tasks flood into
your mind, you can jot them down, put them out of mind
for the time being, and get on with your praying.

A few minutes of physical exercise to get your blood
circulating freely may also enable you to concentrate
better. However, one of the most effective things you
can do is to find a quiet place. This will help concentra-

tion more than any other thing you can do.

Sometimes in our busy, hectic world it is difficult to find such a place. This is especially true if you live in a small apartment, a college dormitory, or a busy household. However, it is essential that you find a quiet time and place to be alone with God. You may have to follow the habit of Jesus, who got up a great while before day and went into a solitary place in order to be alone with God (Mark 1:35). He lived in a much less hectic day than ours. However, he found it necessary to say no to sleep in order to say yes to a quiet time with God. You may have to do the same thing.

You Need a Set Time for Prayer

Daniel prayed three times a day. He made and kept regular appointments with God. You would do well to do the same thing. If our body says to us, "Three times today you shall go with me to eat," why shouldn't we say to our body, "Three times today you shall go with me to pray." We should not look upon prayer as just a routine to be endured. It is not like punching a spiritual time clock, so that we get credit with God. It is rather a means of continual communion with him. That's why we need to make and keep regular appointments in prayer.

The Bible says that we are to pray without ceasing (1 Thess. 5:17). This means that we are to be in an attitude of prayer at all times. There are several things that you can do to help fulfill this teaching.

The psalmist had a habit of praying seven times a day. He said, "Seven times a day do I praise thee"

(Ps. 119:164). That's not a bad habit. You may find it helpful to mark your days into shorter segments so that you might be constantly coming to him in the midst of the activities of life. It can help us live in moment-by-moment fellowship with God. You might pray the first thing on arising in the morning and the last thing before retiring at night. That would be twice. Then you could pray before each meal. That would be five times. Then you could pray at midmorning and at midafternoon. A prayer break, like a coffee break, might give you a spiritual pickup throughout the day. This would be a total of seven times each day.

You might decide to pray every time you miss a green light and are forced to wait at an intersection. That could give you a prayer ministry you've never had before. Besides it would be a whole lot better than fretting and fuming at the loss of time.

Or you might follow the practice of a great business leader, Mr. J. Arthur Rank. He had an elevator straight up to his office, but he didn't use it. He preferred the stairs and he called them his "prayer stairs." In the morning as he walked up he prayed, asking God to guide him in every step he took that day. As he took each step separately and deliberately, he prayed. When he finally arrived, he was really at the top.

In the morning he walked up asking. Then in the evening he walked down, thanking God for the help he had given him that day. Those stairs became about the most important thing in Mr. Rank's life. Having some prayer stairs could be good exercise in more ways than one.

If you are in a car a lot, you might let certain things be prayer reminders to you. When you see a hospital it could remind you to pray for the sick. A funeral home could remind you to pray for the bereaved. A school could remind you to pray for little children. When you see the flag it could remind you to pray for our government. When you see the church it could remind you to pray for the work of God and our missionaries. These reminders could keep us on our spiritual knees throughout the day.

Some people pray while they are in the bathtub. This is a good place to get clean on both the inside and the outside.

However, these expressions of prayer without ceasing are not to be substitutes for a definite time of prayer. Most of the great men of God have had a specific time when they met with the Lord each day. You need to be able to say that you have a definite time of prayer. In setting a time for prayer it is not the amount of time that you set aside that is most important. It is the fact that you discipline yourself to keep the appointment. The amount of time will soon take care of itself. If you establish the discipline of meeting God on a regular basis, you will soon be spending as much time as you need to in prayer.

When is the best time to pray? As I quoted earlier, Jesus had to get up a great while before day to find his time. For David it was also early in the morning. He said, "My voice shalt thou hear in the morning, O LORD; in the morning will I direct my prayer unto thee, and will look up" (Ps. 5:3). The morning hours when people are fresh and can talk to God unhurried will be the best time for prayer. Samuel Chadwick said, "Hurry is the death of prayer." So find a time when you can be fresh and unhurried and keep that regular appointment with God.

You Need to Get on Your Knees

The Bible says that Daniel "kneeled upon his knees." That's a good practice. William Cowper said, "Satan trembles when he sees the weakest saint upon his knees."

No posture is more sacred than another for prayer. In the Scriptures we find people praying in many different postures. There were times when people fell on their faces before God in prayer (2 Sam. 12:16). Paul said, "I will therefore that men pray every where, lifting up holy hands, without wrath and doubting" (1 Tim. 2:8). This is the posture of a little child reaching out to his father in need. This is the posture of opening your hands to God to receive a blessing from him. It's a good posture in prayer.

However, my favorite posture is that of kneeling, which more than anything else suggests the idea of humility. In the first century when people came before an Oriental potentate, they came on their knees. The best way to unload a burden from your back is to go down with it. As you go down on your knees you are better able to release the burden. Prayer is humbling ourselves before God. Prayer is coming before the great king. Prayer is taking our burden to the Lord and leaving it there. Then surely kneeling is the best posture for prayer.

C. S. Lewis, in his book *The Screwtape Letters,* gives emphasis to this. *The Screwtape Letters* is a satire about an old, experienced devil who is trying to teach a young and upcoming devil how to trip up Christians. Screwtape tells the young devil on one occasion that he should never ever tell a Christian that he should not pray. He said they are too smart to fall for that. However, he should tell them that it is not necessary to get on their knees to pray. Tell them that they can pray just as well in bed on their back. And the first thing you will know they will have closed their eyes and gone to sleep and forgotten their prayer life. Satan is too smart to try to divert us from prayer altogether. However, if he can keep us off our knees, he will greatly weaken our prayer life and will soon win the victory over us.

We Need to Do More Than Ask

The verse says that Daniel prayed "and gave thanks." This suggests to us that prayer to Daniel was more than just asking God for things. Understand this, it is not wrong to ask for things. If God is our father, then it is not wrong for us to ask things of him. He tells us, "Or what man is there of you, whom if his son ask bread, will he give him a stone? Or if he ask a fish, will he give him a serpent? If ye then, being evil, know how to give good gifts unto your children, how much more shall your Father which is in heaven give good things to them that ask him?" (Matt. 7:9–11).

But prayer is much more than just asking. The most effective praying begins by confessing what we have done. The Scriptures say, "If I regard iniquity in my heart, the Lord will not hear me" (Ps. 66:18). So we ought to begin by confessing every sin that comes to our mind. It may even help if we make a list of them. Write them down and then read them to God. If we do he will forgive and cleanse us from all unrighteousness (1 John 1:9).

Then we should praise God for who he is. It is well to take some attribute of God such as his love, his knowledge of all things, his great power, or his unchanging nature and praise him for it.

Then we should intercede for other people. The Bible says, "I exhort therefore, that, first of all, supplications, prayers, intercessions, and giving of thanks, be made for all men; For kings, and for all that are in authority; that we may lead a quiet and peaceable life in all godliness and honesty" (1 Tim. 2:1–2). When we intercede for other people we should be very specific in our praying. As Josef Nordenhaug said, "Don't pray for me by simply saying, 'God bless all for whom I should pray.' That's typically American, the wholesale way. But please pray for me personally."

Then, of course, we have a right to ask things for ourselves. We can petition God for our own needs. He teaches us this again and again in Scripture.

Then, as Daniel, we should thank God for what he has done. The Bible teaches us that we should give thanks to

God in everything (1 Thess. 5:18; Ps. 118:1; Phil. 4:6).
Count your blessings and begin to thank God for them. If
you can't think of any blessing, then maybe you ought to
thank God for the fact that he hasn't answered all of your
prayers. Benjamin Franklin said in *Poor Richard's Al-
manac*, "If man could have half his wishes, he would
double his troubles." Most of us have lived long enough
to thank God for not answering all of our prayers. So you
can at least thank him for that.

Finally, prayer should include silence. This is also a
vital part of prayer. The psalmist said, "Be still, and
know that I am God" (Ps. 46:10). We sometimes talk
about dead silence. But to me it is a mistaken figure of
speech because silence is very much alive. Things leap to
your mind out of silence. It is as if all of your senses were
on their tiptoes and there is a faint ringing in your ears
which could be your memory tuning up, humming like a
tightwire. So confess to God where you have failed;
praise God for who he is; intercede to God for the needs
of others; thank God for what he has done; ask God for
what you need; and then be quiet in his presence and
listen for his still, small voice.

In H. G. Wells' *Anne Veronica*, the heroine cries out
during a crisis in her life when things had piled up in
overwhelming amounts, "Oh, God, how I wish I had
been taught to pray!"

You know how to pray. So go to it. Make a prayer list.
Approach God in absolute honesty. Talk in a natural
language. We pray to a living God so pray in a living
language. Pray in Jesus' name. As Billy Sunday said,

"When I go to God, in the name of Jesus Christ, God will stop making worlds to hear me."

And, above all, don't be a dropout. Even if you don't feel that God is listening, keep praying. God's hearing does not depend upon your feelings. He hears you whether you think he does or not. Remember that when you use the hot line to heaven you never get a busy signal. So don't be a prayer dropout. Stay with it and God will bless you with spiritual growth and power.

3
Studying—Six Ways to Study the Bible

A new convert to Christ shared his experience with me. Among his new discoveries was the richness of the Bible. He said, "The Bible is something else. Man, it is some Book." He was right. The Bible is some Book. And every believer needs to make that discovery for himself.

The Bible is the inspired Word of God. It is more than a book of history, ethics, or philosophy. It is God's Word to man. It is the result of God's spirit stirring the hearts and lives of men. When the Holy Spirit moved on the hearts of holy men, they penned the holy Scriptures (2 Pet. 1:21).

Because it is inspired, it is authoritative. It is our accurate guide in belief and practice. As a watch is our authority on time, as a compass is our authority on directions, as a dictionary is our authority on definitions, so the Bible is our authority on what to believe and how to live (2 Tim. 3:16–17).

And it is eternal. Other books come and go, but the Bible is timeless. It is never out-of-date. The grass withereth, and the flower thereof falleth away: But the word of the Lord endureth forever (1 Pet. 1:24–25).

All of this makes the Bible indispensable to the believer. Several analogies tell us why. It is the milk (1 Pet. 2:2) and meat (Heb. 5:14) that help us grow spiritually. It is a lamp to guide us down the path of life (Ps. 119:105). It is a mirror in which we see our true selves (Jas. 1:23). It is a surgeon's knife that lays bare and analyzes our deepest being (Heb. 4:12). And it is a sword with which we defend ourselves against the enemy (Eph. 6:17). The Bible is all this and more. That's why it is a must for every believer.

Two things will help you get the most out of the Bible. One is to avail yourself of the ministry of gifted teachers. The other is to study the Bible on your own.

The New Testament recognizes and emphasizes that the Spirit of God equips certain people for a teaching ministry. They make real to our hearts the truth of Scripture. Utilize the ministry of these people whom God has gifted for teaching his word (Eph. 4:11). You can get this help through regular church services, conferences, books, and through tapes. You need this help. Don't try to be independent of all human help.

But this alone is not enough. You need to search the Scriptures on your own. No one can spoon-feed you to maturity. You must spend time studying privately to get the help you need.

We must rid ourselves of the idea that the Bible is a dark and difficult book. God wrote it for ordinary people like us. And we can understand it if we study it correctly. So one of the most pressing needs for all believers is to learn how to study the Bible.

The Bereans are a good example. The Bible says this

about them: "And the brethren immediately sent away
Paul and Silas by night unto Berea: who coming thither
went into the synagogue of the Jews. These were more
noble than those in Thessalonica, in that they received
the word with all readiness of mind, and searched the
scriptures daily, whether those things were so. Therefore many of them believed; also of honourable women
which were Greeks, and of men, not a few" (Acts 17:
10–12).

Paúl had just preached in Thessalonica where he es-
tablished a church. Then he was run out of town by the
narrow-minded, unbelieving Jews. So he came to Berea
and began to preach. There he found quite a different
attitude. Luke says of them, "These were more noble
than those in Thessalonica." The word "noble" is very
suggestive. It has nothing to do with their ancestors. Nor
does it have anything to do with their birth. It rather has
reference to their character of disposition. The best English interpretation of this word is "liberal" in the sense
that they were free from prejudice. These Bereans were
to be contrasted with those in Thessalonica who were so
bigoted that they would not listen to the truth. They had
closed their minds to the possibility of there being any
truth outside of Judaism. So they refused to hear what
the apostle Paul had to say and they drove him out of
town.

But when Paul got to Berea, he found the people free
from this kind of prejudice and bigotry. With commend-
able open-mindedness they eagerly listened to what he
had to say. Then they brought his message to the Scrip-

tures, their final court appeal, and searched them out to see if they were true. They did more than read the Scriptures. They examined, investigated, and sifted through them. They discovered that what Paul was saying in his sermons and what God was saying in his Scriptures were exactly the same. Then they readily opened their hearts and received Jesus Christ as their Savior. They became converts to Christianity.

The Bereans were people with open minds, open Bibles, and open hearts. Their openness led to an open response to the gospel. They stand throughout all of the ages as an example of how to study the Bible, either by direct statement or by implications. They teach us much about good Bible study practices.

Use a Modern Translation

If we are to get the most out of Bible study, then we must use a version that is written in modern English. Many people have problems relating the Bible to everyday life because its words in the King James Version are different from those we use in everyday life. Our newspapers aren't written in King James English. Very few couples fight or make love in King James English. So why should we read the Bible or pray in King James English?

The King James Version of the Bible is the most beautiful translation ever made. And it will always be a favorite translation among most people. But many of the words are three-and-one-half centuries out of date. It was translated from the Greek into the English in 1611.

It is called the King James Version because it was translated at the command of King James I of England. And it was translated into the common language of the people of that day. However, today we no longer say thee and thou in our ordinary conversation. And many of the words used in it are no longer used. So the Bible seems confusing.

Unfortunately through the years many people have come to associate those words and other sixteenth century words with holy language. They are not holy language at all. They are simply the language of the street three hundred and fifty years ago. So for the best results study the Bible in modern language. Better still, read it in several different translations and the Bible will come alive.

Follow a Plan of Bible Study

You need a plan of Bible study. Many people approach their Bible study too haphazardly. This has its dangers. I once heard of a man who followed the practice of opening the Bible at random each day, and finding a verse of Scripture he considered that was God's message to him for that day. One day following his procedure, he opened the Bible to the verse that said, "[Judas] and went and hanged himself" (Matt. 27:5). Assuming that he had made a mistake, he closed the Bible, opened it again and found another verse. This verse said, "Go, and do thou likewise" (Luke 10:37). From that day forward he decided that there was bound to be a better way of studying the Scriptures.

I hope you have discovered that there is a better way to study the Bible, too. There are many different plans you can use to help you make your Bible study more valuable. The particular plan you use is not so important. The important thing is that you have some plan.

One plan is to begin with the Gospel of Mark. This is a short, fast-moving account of the life of Christ. Remember as you read that Jesus teaches us by what he does as well as by what he says.

Next read the Gospel of John. It is a different arrangement of the life and teaching of Jesus and an in-depth study of his divinity. It gives special emphasis to his discourses and conversations.

Then read the book of Acts. This is a history of the church and the work of the apostles from the time Christ ascended into heaven until the gospel was spread throughout the known world.

Next read the books following Acts. These are letters written by the apostle Paul to churches and individuals. The name of the book tells us the person or church for whom the letter was intended. These letters were intended to teach Christians of all ages what to believe and how to live.

Then begin to read in the Old Testament. It is a record of God's dealings with man, especially as he prepares them for the coming of his son, Jesus Christ. Start by reading the practical wisdom of Proverbs and the devotional thoughts of the Psalms.

Then go back and read the books of history from Genesis through Esther (be careful not to get bogged down in genealogies or Old Testament laws).

Finally, close out by studying the fiery sermons of the prophets.

Another plan is to study the Bible by themes or by characters. Pick some subject like faith, prayer, or love and study all the Scriptures in the Bible that relate to this subject. Or pick a character in the Bible such as David, Barnabas, or Andrew and read those passages that deal with him. This kind of study can be fruitful in giving you an overview of some particular subject or character. A good concordance will be of help in this kind of study.

Another helpful way to study the Bible is to learn the date, author, and background of a particular book. To know the author, date, and circumstances behind a book makes its message come alive.

When we have an illness, we don't just go to the cabinet and get some medicine without any regard for the label or date, writer of the prescription, or conditions under which it was originally given. This kind of information is also vital to understanding the message of a book in the Bible. You can find this information in a good Bible handbook, a Bible dictionary, or a commentary. For example, in one of his writings Paul says, "I have learned, in whatsoever state I am, therewith to be content" (Phil. 4:11). That's a wonderful statement. But if you know the background to the writing of it, it becomes ever more meaningful. If Paul were sitting in a penthouse by the Mediterranean Sea when he wrote those words, they would have one meaning. But since he was in a jail in Rome when he penned them, they have an entirely different meaning. So knowing the background can help you in your Bible study.

Read the Bible Daily

The Bereans searched the Scriptures "daily" to see whether those things were so. There is no substitute for a day-by-day studying of God's Word. I have discovered in my own life that the things that are left to chance are usually left out. So we need to have a regular schedule of Bible study. We need to treat the Bible like food. We don't eat just once a week, or even once a day. We eat at regular intervals. We also need to take in spiritual nourishment at regular intervals.

Set aside a regular time for daily reading, however brief, choosing a time when your mind is fresh and receptive. I believe that the morning is better than night. It's better to live on the Bible than to sleep on it.

"Make it the first morning business of your life," says Ruskin, "to understand some part of the Bible clearly and make it your daily business to obey it in all that you do understand."

Leland Wang was a dedicated and effective Christian from China. He once told how he had tried on many occasions to have a regular devotional life, but all his attempts failed. Finally, after years and years of trying, he found a successful method of Bible study and devotional life. He offered these suggestions for us.

1. Carry your Bible with you at all times. Then while you are waiting on a bus or for a doctor's appointment or

some such time, you can read your Bible in your spare moments.

2. Adopt a motto such as "No Bible-no breakfast." Since most of us like to eat, we will always manage to study the Bible so that we can have something to eat. He suggested that this motto was not a law to bind him, but a guide to remind him that man does not live by bread alone. We all need that reminder.

3. Have a plan of Bible study. His plan was to read two chapters from the Old Testament, two chapters from the New Testament, five psalms, and one chapter of Proverbs each day. This way he read the New Testament three times a year, the Old Testament once a year, and Psalms and Proverbs once every month. He used the book of Proverbs as his spiritual calendar, reading one chapter each day. He read each day the chapter number that corresponded with that day of the month. That way he always had his spiritual calendar with him.

No Bible study can be interesting if it is not regular. Let's determine in God's strength to trample under our feet the laziness that kills our Bible study.

The Bible requires serious attention and diligent, systematic, and regular study if it is to be enjoyed. We must decide whether it's worth it or not.

Read the Bible Carefully

The Bereans "searched" the Scriptures. This means that they examined, investigated, and sifted through the Scriptures. We are not to look upon Bible reading as we do assigned reading for a college course. The object is

not just to get through. We are to read the Bible slowly
and let everything in God's Word soak into us. There is
no merit in having read the Bible through two or three
times unless God's message has penetrated our hearts.
The purpose is not for us to get through the Bible, but
rather for the Bible to get through us.

The Bible is not for speed reading. Aldous Huxley in
Ends and Means told how training is needed before one
can fully savor anything.

I defy anyone to pick anything really significant out of
a book like the Bible by speed-reading. It would be like
playing a Beethoven record at the wrong speed.

You remember the story of Elijah's servant who went
once to look into the hills for the army of God and saw
nothing. He came back and told his master and was sent
to look again. Seven times Elijah sent him to look. Finally on the seventh time he saw the host of God surrounding their village. So you may look lightly upon
Scriptures and see nothing. Meditate upon it again and
again and you shall see a light like the light of the sun.
Too often we look lightly at the Word of God and see
nothing. You may want to read the Bible with a pencil in
your hand, marking key verses of Scripture that you will
want to go back and reread later.

One of the problems you are apt to face in your Bible
reading is a wandering mind. If you mark your reading it
will help your concentration.

One of the best exercises you can perform is copying
passages that especially appeal to you. This helps you
retain truth to an unusual degree. Or, as you study a

passage you might ask: Is there a promise to claim? Is there a command to obey? Is there a doctrine to believe? Is there a sin to avoid? Is there an example to follow? And then note which it is in the margin of your Bible.

We should do more than just read the Bible. We should memorize it. We should hide it in our hearts. Memorization is not as dependent on our ability as upon our interest. We all have a far greater ability to remember than we think. If someone gave you one hundred dollars for every verse you memorized, you would memorize quite a few. You just need to be motivated. You can memorize verses while you are shaving, while you are driving, while you are washing the dishes, or doing many other things. The Word of God stored in your heart will be an invaluable source of guidance in the days ahead.

Read the Bible Prayerfully

We never know who wrote most of the books that we read. And in fact, it is not necessary that we do. We can understand the author's message, receive his truth, and benefit from his thinking without ever having met or known him. However, the Bible is exactly the opposite. In order to understand it, benefit from it, and get the most out of it, we must know the author himself.

Since men are spiritually blind and dead, they must be regenerated to understand the spiritual message of the Bible. Men may admire its literary beauty, or its historical accuracy, and yet miss the real truth of it. Bible study is like looking at anything else. What a man sees depends primarily on where he is. If we are standing in faith and humility, we are more apt to see God's truth.

It takes the eyes of an artist to appreciate good art. It takes the ears of a musician to understand fine music. And it takes the ears and eyes and heart of a soul open to the spirit of God to understand the wonders of God's Word.

Bertram Russell was a great philosopher. He was a descendant of one of England's most distinguished families. He was a versatile and brilliant scholar, author, and winner of the Nobel prize for literature in 1950. Yet this man with all of his brilliance had been consistently antagonistic toward Christianity. One of his works, *Why I Am Not A Christian*, indicates that he obviously did not have an understanding of the Word of God. To be sure he understands some things intellectually. But the spiritual message of the Bible is foreign to him. I mentioned earlier that the Bible is inspired. Inspiration is two-fold. It was given by inspiration. And it is understood and received by inspiration too. It is only as the Holy Spirit, who led in the writing of this book, interprets it to us that its full meaning comes to us. So we need to read the Bible prayerfully.

Read It Obediently

The Bereans were open-minded people. They were ready to learn from God's Word. We do not read the Bible just to learn facts, but to expose ourselves to the living God. This means that we read the Bible with a willingness to change. We read it so we can do what God wants us to do. If we can read it as the Bereans did, free from prejudices, free from bigotry, free from preconceived ideas, then God will be able to speak to us from his Word. When they saw the truth, they obeyed it. They believed on Christ.

Don't worry about the parts of the Bible you don't understand. You'll understand enough to keep you busy all of your life. As someone has said, "Many things in the Bible I cannot understand; many things in the Bible I only think I understand; but there are many things in the Bible I cannot misunderstand. And what I do understand I am to obey." The aim of Bible study is not primarily to build up a reservoir of knowledge, but to conform the reader to the image of God's Son.

So you must appropriate the Bible to life. Mix it with faith and act upon it. There are over seven thousand promises in the Bible. They are like seven thousand bags of cement that must be mixed with faith and action to fulfill their purpose. Paul warns us not to be overly concerned with debatable details and puzzling problems (Titus 3:9). Satan delights to see us major on minors or quibble over details that contribute nothing to a closer walk with God.

Sometimes we get disturbed because we don't understand everything in the Bible. But we can't expect it to read like a ninety-five cent paperback. This book was written by God. How then can we pick it up and read it as though some mere men had penned it. It takes much thought and prayer and study and the illumination of the Holy Spirit for its truth to come through to us. However, if we persist, God will more and more open our minds so that we can understand this book.

Obey God's Word and you will begin to understand it more. There are ABC's to Christianity as to anything. When you were in school, you learned your ABC's, and soon you could understand things you couldn't when you started out. Obedience to God's Word produces the same enlarged understanding.

You have no right to expect any further revelation until you have decided to attend to the ones you already know. The neglected duty becomes an obstacle blocking our view to see more.

It is a sobering thought to realize that we will be the same in five years as we are today except for the books we read and the people we meet. Take care to see that you are in close contact with the best of both. And the best of the best books is the Bible. Follow the example of the Bereans and search the Scriptures daily.

4
Worshiping—Why Attend Church?

While having lunch with a free-lance writer who had recently been converted from Judaism to Christianity, our conversation turned to the church. He said, "The church just doesn't do much for me. I go there with a thousand other people, and somebody gets up and tells me how to live. I don't need that. Jesus has already told me how to live. He changed my life and he is guiding me day by day. I simply do not need the church." I am hearing more and more talk like that today. It is talk of a churchless Christianity.

The Bible knows nothing of that. Christianity is to be lived in fellowship with other believers. It is never lived in isolation. Anyone serious about living for Christ and growing to spiritual maturity needs the church.

God recognized that every believer needs worship, inspiration, and fellowship in order to grow to full spiritual maturity and that's why he gave us the church in the first place.

The Bible makes this clear when it says: "Let us draw near with a true heart in full assurance of faith, having our hearts sprinkled from an evil conscience, and our bodies washed with pure water. Let us hold fast the profession of our faith without wavering; (for he is faithful that promised;) and let us consider one another to provoke unto love and to good works: Not forsaking the assembling of ourselves together, as the manner of some is; but exhorting one another: and so much the more, as ye see the day approaching" (Heb. 10:22–25).

The basic exhortations of this passage are that we draw near to God, that we hold on to our profession of faith, and that we provoke one another unto the highest kind of living. But if we do this we must not neglect church attendance as some are doing. Obviously there were some in the first century who had already given up the practice of meeting together regularly with other Christians. We aren't sure why. Maybe it was out of fear of persecution. The cost of being a Christian was exceedingly high in that day. When a person became a Christian he laid his life on the line for Jesus Christ.

Maybe it was out of conceit. Perhaps some of these people thought they had advanced spiritually beyond the need of further teaching and fellowship and inspiration.

Maybe it was out of indifference. Maybe they had lost interest in the things of the Spirit. They had been recaptured by the world, and had ceased to hunger and thirst after righteousness. For whatever reason, some had forsaken the assembling of themselves together. With this neglect they were heading for spiritual disaster. The writer felt a need to warn others not to follow their example. If we are to live for God and grow to maturity, we must be faithful in church attendance also. Why is church attendance so important? Why should we go to church?

Make no mistake about it; we do not attend church to score points with God. There are no Brownie points with him. God does not check roll every Sunday to see if we are present. And there will be no perfect attendance awards in heaven. We go to church for what we get out of it. We go for worship, for inspiration, and for fellowship. And if we don't get these things when we go to church, there is either something wrong with us, or there's something wrong with the church. Either it's not doing its job or we are not open and receptive to it.

There are reasons for everyone to attend church. Let's examine them.

We Go to Church to Worship God

We are told first to "draw near" to God. Where could you find a better definition of worship than that? Worship is drawing near to God. It is entering into his presence.

Worship is a recognition and acknowledgment of that which is of supreme worth in life. Everything can't be first in your life. Something or someone has to be most important. Whatever is of supreme value to us is what we worship.

Everyone worships someone or something. Some people worship (that is, place supreme worth on) their career, others worship material possessions, and still others worship pleasure. We Christians place our supreme value on God. He's most important to us.

Worship then is a time when we recognize and ac-

knowledge God as supreme in our lives and thus we get
our life values in perspective. In our hectic world it's so
easy to get values twisted and confused. T. S. Eliot said
that in flying across the Atlantic it took his soul three
days to catch up with his body. Worship is that pause
that allows the physical and spiritual to get back into
proper relationship.

I once pastored in a beautiful central Texas town that
had a large hill overlooking the city and my church.
Occasionally after a hectic day, I would climb that hill
and sit there and try to re-collect my thoughts. There,
overlooking the city and my church, things looked different. In the maze below I was almost overwhelmed.
The problems looked insurmountable. From above they
seemed different.

Worship is like that. It is climbing into God's presence
and looking at life from above. It's getting life back into
perspective. It's getting our values straight again. We all
need that. Of course we can worship God anywhere and
anytime. But the fact is, we most often worship God in
church.

We Go to Church to Get Inspired

The author of Hebrews writes, "Let us hold fast the
profession of our faith without wavering" (v. 23). Our
profession of faith is the confession we made when we
received Christ as our Savior and committed our lives to
him. The encouragement is to "hold fast" to it.

Faith is not a luxury item in life. We are what we
believe. What we believe, what we accept in our deepest

being, determines what we are and how we behave. So our faith is not optional in life. It is standard equipment. Of all people, Christians have something to believe.

. We believe in the God who made heaven and earth. We believe in the God who knows us and cares about us as a father cares about a child. We believe in Christ who gave his life for our sins. By believing on him we can be brought into a right relationship with God. We believe in the Holy Spirit who dwells within every believer to give us victory in life. That doesn't mean we don't have problems and pitfalls and difficulties. It means he is there to strengthen us, to walk with us, and to sustain us in the midst of them. And we have a hope that when we die there will be a resurrection and a heaven. Of all the people on this earth who have something to believe and a profession to make, it is the people of God.

Now the writer says, "Hold on to what you believe." Do you know why he was saying that? Because there are lots of things and lots of people who try to shake you loose from your faith. Sickness, death, failure, temptation, doubts, and even success can all be shaking experiences.

If I associate with people of faith, I am encouraged to hang on to mine in spite of these shakings. I catch people's spirit the same way I catch their colds, by getting near them. If I stay near people with faith, my faith is strengthened also.

We have three bicycles at my house and it is a full-time job to keep them running. One problem I have had with one of them lately is a slow leak in the tire. I pump up the tire with air and in two or three days it is flat again. It leaks. My faith is the same way. It has a slow leak in it also. And if I don't get pumped up about every seven days, I go flat spiritually. That's one reason why God said, "Remember the sabbath day to keep it holy." He knew we were weak and we need to be pumped up at least once a week. You need to be encouraged to hang on to your profession of faith. Through preaching, teaching, singing, praying, and just meeting together we do this.

You have made your profession of faith and it is important to you, but the shakings are going to come and you are going to need some inspiration and some help to hang on. That's what the church is all about.

We Go to Church for Fellowship

Finally, we go to church for fellowship. The writer says, "Let us consider one another, to provoke unto love and good works" (v. 24). The word "consider" means to give attention to, to fix one's eyes upon. The word "provoke" usually carries with it the idea of causing irritation. But it does not always. It can also mean to stimulate and to excite. We are told to fix our eyes upon one another to stimulate and to excite one another to love and to good works.

We need to attend church not only to strengthen our faith so we can hang on to what we have professed a little longer, but to encourage one another to love and to good works. We go to church to encourage one another to the highest kind of living.

There is encouragement for the lowest kind of living

everywhere we turn. Young people in school are encouraged to live the lowest kind of life. The most debased kind of talking and thinking are found at school. And at work, how much encouragement do you get to live the worst kind of life? Usually a great deal. There ought to be some place you can go and get encouragement to live the highest kind of life. The church is really the only place I know where we can get this kind of encouragement.

If you have chosen the Christian life-style, you need the association and encouragement of people with similar convictions. There are some people it's easy to be good around. And there are some people it's easy to be bad around. The church should be a place to find those people that it's easy to be good around—people who bring out the best in you. Sam Jones said, "You can't run with dogs without getting fleas on you." Choose your friends well. They can be the difference between victory and defeat in life.

From Watergate came the sad story of a promising young man, Jeb Stuart McGruder, who gave every evidence of having a tremendous political future. The editor of a newsmagazine wrote this sad epitaph over his career. "He had developed everything except the kind of character to withstand temptation at the highest level of life." Many people are like that. They develop beauty and charm and business skills and social abilities. They develop everything except the kind of character that can withstand temptation. How tragic.

We need to keep coming together as the people of God. We come together so that we can encourage and inspire one another to the highest kind of living. We need to help develop in each other the kind of character to withstand temptation. That's not a job for the preacher only. Every believer is to be an encourager, an inspirer.

One of the greatest compliments that was ever paid to any man was the compliment paid to Job by one of his friends. He said, "Thy words have upholden him that was falling, and thou hast strengthened the feeble knees" (Job 4:4). Moffatt translates that verse, "Your words have kept men on their feet." Isn't that great? Wouldn't you like for people to say, "His words have kept me on my feet. My knees were about to buckle under; I was about to give up, about to quit, about to throw in the towel, about to surrender, about to yield to moral temptation, and his words kept me on my feet."

That's what the church is all about. You don't go to church just to hear someone tell you how to live, as my writer friend suggested. You go to encourage others and get encouraged to the highest kind of living—to love.

That makes church attendance worthwhile for all of us. It's a place to get life back into perspective and see God as God. It's a place to be encouraged to hang on to what you have already professed to believe. And it's a place where you can meet people who will love you and accept you and will help you stay on your feet.

Don't neglect the church.

5
Living—Being a Christian Where You Are

In most modern churches the entire operation points to a great climax on Sunday morning. That is to say, almost everything they do during the week (study, preparation, visitation, and promotion) is pointed to Sunday morning. And so, when churches come together, the service has something of the atmosphere of a highly advertised athletic event. The spectators have come to see the show and the performers have come to perform. Then at 12:00 o'clock, the whistle blows and the act is over and the spectators go home for another week.

I suppose that preachers are more responsible for this than anyone else. But it really has a detrimental effect because it causes Christianity to degenerate into just a Sunday observance. We have a one-day-a-week religion. The poet had this in mind when he said,

"They go to church on Sunday,
They'll be all right on Monday,
It's just a little habit they've acquired."

Now this is the exact opposite of how it was in the New Testament world. Then, the week was not used to pre-

58

pare for Sunday; Sunday was used to prepare for the rest of the week. The people of God came to church on the Lord's Day to gain insight, inspiration, and encouragement. They sought help to guide them and sustain them as they lived for Christ throughout the week. To those early disciples Christianity was an everyday affair.

The apostle Paul advocates this kind of Christianity. He wrote: "But as God hath distributed to every man, as the Lord hath called every one, so let him walk. And so ordain I in all churches. Let every man abide in the same calling wherein he was called. Brethren, let every man, wherein he is called, therein abide with God" (1 Cor. 7:17,20,24).

The Living Bible expresses it more clearly. It says, "So, dear brothers, whatever situation a person is in when he becomes a Christian, let him stay there, for now the Lord is there to help him" (1 Cor. 7:24,TLB).

Corinth was one of the most immoral cities of all time. Its very name was synonymous with debauchery. In that wicked place some people became followers of Christ and were seeking to live the Christian life. They had come out of paganism, and in many instances their husbands or wives had not been converted to Christianity. They were still pagans, involved in pagan practices and religion. Some of these Christians were thinking, "If I could get out of these circumstances, I could become a better Christian. It would be much easier for me to live for Jesus Christ if I were no longer married." So some of them were getting divorces.

Some had at one time been Jews. As a part of their

Jewish religion they had been circumcised. Now they were regretting that. They were wishing they did not have that mark of Judaism. They were thinking, "If I could change my outward circumstances, then I think I could be a better Christian." Many of these Christians were slaves. They were owned by somebody else. The economy of the Roman world was built on slavery. Many of those who were converted to Christianity were slaves. They were thinking, "If I weren't a slave, if I didn't have to do what my boss told me to do, then I could be a Christian." They were thinking, "If I could just have a different set of circumstances in my life, then I could be a much better Christian."

So Paul wrote this passage to say "Be a Christian where you are." If you were married when you became a Christian, then stay married and be a Christian in that marriage. If you were a slave when you became a Christian, don't make your primary objective to become free. Stay a slave and be a Christian in that household. Be a Christian where you are! Paul is saying that it is not basically the work of Christ to give a man a new life, but rather to make his old life new.

It is not the primary function of Christ to change man's circumstances, but rather to change the man. Then he goes back into the same old circumstances a new and different person. When a man becomes a Christian, he still lives in the same house with the same wife in the same neighborhood. He still works with the same people in the same office. The student still goes to the same school or he still plays on the same football team. The wife still has to manage the same household. When you become a Christian the only thing that is changed is *you.* Therefore, your primary objective should not be to try to change your circumstances. Rather your objective should be to live for Jesus Christ where you are.

We need to be a Christian where we live, where we work, and where we spend our leisure time. If we cannot be a Christian in all these places, then something is wrong with our Christianity. The answer is not just to find a new surrounding and a new environment. The answer is in that old surrounding and in that old environment. The answer is to bring the principles of Jesus Christ to bear and to live for him there.

All believers, young and old, need this encouragement.

Be a Christian Where You Live

What kind of home do you have? What are the circumstances that surround your home life? What kind of people do you live with? Are they congenial? Are they easy to live with? Are they thoughtful and loving and happy? Are they selfish and grouchy? Are they always complaining? What kind of person do you live with? Or, let me ask you something about your children. What kind of children do you have? Are they loving? Are they obedient? Are they dependable, or are they everything except dependable? Young people, let me ask you about your parents. What kind of parents do you have? Are they always nagging? Are they always complaining? Do they trust you? Do they respect your rights? What kind of parents do you have?

Regardless of the circumstances of your home life, Paul says, "Be a Christian where you live."

Now, admittedly, it is a whole lot easier to be a Christian if you live with the right kind of person. If the person is congenial, then it is a lot easier for you to live for Jesus Christ in that environment. If your parents are understanding, sympathetic, and communicative, it is easier to live for Christ in that environment. But the Bible does not exempt us from living for Jesus Christ just because our environment isn't what it ought to be.

Many times God's people are called upon to live in difficult circumstances. There are some people who just aren't easy to live with. Charles Laughton was once asked in a radio interview if he would ever consider marrying again. The question was hypothetical inasmuch as Laughton was happily married to Elsa Lancaster. He answered that he would never contemplate such a step. Pushed for a reason, he said that a man puts his best foot forward during courtship and takes care not to reveal his poorer qualities. Then after marriage his real self emerges day by day and the wife has to make the best of it. And then he said thoughtfully, "I don't think I'd ever put a woman through that again."

Men are sometimes hard to live with. Men often really put women through it. After a long study of myself and my fellow males, I have concluded that man is an irrational being who is always demanding a hotel atmosphere at home and a home atmosphere in a hotel.

Women can be hard to live with, too. Proverbs 21:9

says, "It is better to dwell in a corner of the housetop, than with a brawling woman in a wide house." In the same chapter, verse 19 says, "It is better to dwell in the wilderness, than with a contentious and an angry woman."

Young people can be hard to live with—and parents, too. But the answer is always the same. Don't try to escape. Stay where you are and be a Christian there.

It may be difficult. It may be unpleasant. But there we ought to practice the love and the patience and the forgiveness of Jesus Christ. If a person is not a Christian where he lives, it's doubtful that he is a Christian at all.

Be a Christian Where You Work

What about your job—what's it like? Do you spend your time pumping gasoline, or do you spend your time burning it up on the highways? Do you spend your time pushing a pencil, or do you spend your time pushing a laboring crew? Do you spend your time out in the open air, or do you spend your time in a smoke-filled office? What about the circumstances of your job? Are the people around you Christians? Or are they people who try to outdo one another in their filthy language, dirty jokes, and immoral lives? Paul said, that regardless of the circumstances, you ought to stay and show people what Jesus Christ can do in your life.

Some people say that Christianity and business don't mix. If that be true, there is something wrong with either your Christianity or your business. One of them needs to change. Real Christianity ought not only to mix

in our everyday life, but it ought also to make us better
workers. Repeatedly the New Testament talks about
labor and a Christian's responsibility. It says that if a man
knows Jesus Christ as his Savior, then he ought to be a
better worker. He ought to be more conscientious. He
ought to be more thoughtful. He ought to be more
diligent. And he ought to carry on his work as though
Jesus Christ were his shop foreman.

When we become a Christian, Jesus Christ becomes
the supreme Master of our life. He is as concerned about
the way you do your work as he is about the way you
teach your Sunday School class. He never segments your
life to say here is your religious responsibility, here is
your vocation, and never the twain shall meet. Jesus is
equally concerned about every part of your life.

A Christian can be a Christian in almost any kind of
work. I know of only two kinds of work that a Christian
ought not to be involved in. One is a parasite business,
such as gambling, that preys on the weaknesses of
people. A Christian should get out of that kind of work.
And a Christian should not be involved in any kind of
dishonest endeavor. If there is cheating or dishonesty
going on, then the Christian should not be a part of it.
But beyond that, no matter how menial it may be, work
has dignity. Do you doubt that? Then let all the
preachers and all the garbage collectors go on strike at
once and see which one is missed first.

Somebody said, "There's nothing wrong with dirt on a
man's hands so long as it is the kind he can wash off." A
man can have dignity in his labor if he brings the princi-

ples of Jesus Christ to bear upon it. So Paul said to us as Christians that we should take the gospel of Jesus Christ with us. We need to take Christ with us into that office, into the department store, into the classroom, or onto the football field. Wherever we work and earn our livelihood, and wherever we play, we ought to live for Jesus Christ. Be a Christian where you are.

Be a Christian Where You Spend Your Leisure Time

Where do you spend your leisure time? I hope you have some. You need it. It's tremendously important. A recent news article on stress pointed out that every person needs some recreational outlet for a healthy and happy life. The activity may be many things—tennis, golf, bowling, fishing. In the midst of the pressures of our world today, a person needs a change of pace occasionally.

Some unknown poet expressed it this way:

> If you keep your nose to the grindstone rough,
> And you hold it there long enough,
> You soon will say, 'There's no such thing
> As a babbling brook or birds that sing.'
> These three things will all your life compose;
> Just you, the stone, and a ground-down nose.

That's the way it is in life. A man needs to take some leisure time. If you don't, you do it to your own detriment.

Paul said that wherever you spend your leisure time,

you should seek to live for Jesus Christ. Live for him on
the golf course, at the bowling alley, at the lake, in a
garden, or wherever. He is as vitally concerned about
your recreational life as he is about any other part of your
life. Never does our Lord say, "This is off limits. This is
of no concern to me." He cares greatly about every
segment of our lives. The Christian can never abandon
life altogether. We can't live in a vacuum. God expects
us to be involved in the business world. He expects us to
be involved in the social world, and in recreational life.
But he expects us to live for him while we are there.

In 1947 an American expedition discovered an ancient
monastery in the wild mountains and desert of the Sinai
Peninsula. It had been there since A.D. 340. They found
there Father Pachomius, who had not set foot outside
the walls in fifty years. He had never heard of World War
I or II. God's not interested in that kind of religion. He's
not interested in the kind of existence that separates us
from the rest of the world. We have to be involved in all
kinds of activities. We are to be in the world, but not of
the world. And while we are here, we are to live for
Jesus Christ.

So Paul said that wherever you live, or work, or spend
your leisure time, make your life count for Jesus Christ.
Paul said, "For me to live is Christ." He meant that
wherever I am and whatever I am doing, it is Christ
living all over again. He meant in the locker room, in the
smoke-filled office, or wherever. For me to live is for
Christ to be there and for Christ to live his life all over
again. It is possible by the grace of God to be a Christian

where you are.

One of the greatest Christians of all time was Booker T. Washington. He was born a slave on a plantation in Virginia. Until he was emancipated, his life was wretched and miserable. He never knew his father. He never slept on a bed until he was emancipated. He slept on the floor of a little shack, seventeen feet by fourteen feet. It had no windows, just holes in the side of the wall. He seldom had enough to eat. But in that wretched, miserable condition as a slave, Booker T. Washington learned to love Jesus Christ.

When he was finally emancipated, he went to work in a new and fresh way for God. He founded the Tuskegee Institute which now has over 2,600 students and an endowment of over $2,000,000. It is one of the greatest Negro schools in this country. He became an adviser to presidents and a friend to all men. He could have said, "If I hadn't been a slave, if I could have had a better education, if I could have had a better environment, if I could have had better circumstances, I could have done something for Christ." But he didn't say that. He became a Christian where he was. He stayed there and made the best of bad circumstances and God blessed him and honored him. That's what I am suggesting to you.

Young people, husbands, wives, employers, employees, sports fans, or whoever you may be, stay where you are. The answer is not to find a new environment. The answer is to become a new person in Jesus Christ. Then be a Christian where you live, where you work, and where you spend your leisure time.

6
Discovering—Sense and Nonsense About Spiritual Gifts

In studying the history of the early church there seems to be little doubt that when a person was converted he was immediately taught two things. First, he was taught that the Holy Spirit had imparted to him new life in Christ. Then he was taught that the Holy Spirit had also equipped him with spiritual gifts which he was responsible for discovering, developing, and dedicating to God's service.

What is a spiritual gift? The Greek word means an endowment-given grace. A spiritual gift is an endowment, an ability, that equips us to do the work of God. It is an extraordinary ability given a man that he could never acquire himself. He could never attain it alone. It is like becoming a super athlete, or a concert pianist, or an outstanding speaker, or writer.

One person might practice the piano all of his life and never excel at it while another masters it with comparative ease. Another might practice speaking and never move an audience, while someone else can step forward and at once hold the audience in rapt attention. Another might toil a lifetime to learn how to put his thoughts down on paper in an intelligent way and never do it. From someone else, words may seem to flow like a river. Some people are naturally gifted with intelligence, stamina, and ability, but these must not be considered as just natural abilities. They are gifts from God.

William Faulkner, a genius and an outstanding writer, wrote to a friend in 1953, "Now, I realize for the first time what an amazing gift I had: uneducated in every formal sense, . . ., let alone literary companions, yet to have made the things I made. I don't know where it came from." I do! His gift came from the same Holy Spirit who gives men all the gifts they possess.

The New Testament teaches us several basic truths about spiritual gifts. First, the Holy Spirit gives to every one of us some gift that we are to use in the service of God (1 Cor. 12:7). This is a part of the strategy for his church. He distributes to every believer the gift he wishes him to have. We do not earn these gifts. Nor do we deserve the gifts. We simply receive them from the Holy Spirit.

The apostle Paul often used the analogy of a human body to describe the church (1 Cor. 12:12–27). The church as a whole is the body of Christ and the members individually are parts of that body. As every part of our body is important, so every member of the body of Christ is important. We each are different and distinct and have our own unique function. Yet we are fit together to make one body. And each part of our body is gifted for some service. No one has all the gifts. But everyone has at least one gift. And there are no useless parts in the body of Christ.

All the gifts the Holy Spirit gives are service gifts. They are given for the common good. They are given for the exclusive use of ministry. He never gives a gift to satisfy our ego. Nor does he give a gift just to make us feel good. He gives us gifts to make us useful in his kingdom's service. They are for the benefit of the church. They are for the benefit of the progress of God's kingdom on earth (1 Cor. 12:7).

All of these gifts are to promote unity. The idea of the church as a body and the members as part of that body suggest both diversity and unity. As a part of the body we ought to work in harmony with one another. Several years ago I sprained my ankle. It hurt and swelled up. The rest of my body was so concerned about it that I sat up all night with it. That's the way it is with the body of Christ. There is diversity and yet there is unity (1 Cor. 12:26).

But beware! These gifts can be neglected or perverted. Paul told us that the church in Corinth was misusing the gifts that God had given to them (1 Cor. 12–14). He wrote to Timothy on two separate occasions concerning his spiritual gifts. He said, "Neglect not the gift that is in thee" (1 Tim. 4:14). Obviously Timothy was not using the gift that the Holy Spirit had given him. If Timothy could do that, you and I can do it also.

Then he wrote later, "Wherefore I put thee in remembrance that thou stir up the gift of God, which is within thee" (2 Tim. 1:6). The words "stir up" literally mean "to fan again to flames." It is the idea of coals that have grown cold and gray because the fire has died out. Timothy had grown cold and indifferent in the use of his spiritual gifts and needed to fan them to a flame again. God had given him the gifts, but he was neglecting them, allowing them to grow cold. You and I may do the same thing.

There is a difference between the gifts of the Spirit and the fruit of the Spirit. The gifts of the Spirit have to do with ability. They have to do with equipping us for service. The fruit of the Spirit has to do with character (Gal. 5:22–23). When our lives are yielded to the Holy Spirit, he develops a Christlike character in us. At the same time he gives us the special endowments and abilities to carry on his work more effectively.

It is the special assignment of the pastor to help you discover and develop your spiritual gift. Paul told us that God has given various officers in a church such as apostles, prophets, evangelists, pastors, and teachers to help develop us so that we can do the work of the ministry (Eph. 4:11–12). The pastor is not to do all the work. He is to train and help others to do the work. He is gifted for that (Eph. 4:11–13).

The Bible speaks of spiritual gifts often. They are mentioned in 1 Cor. 12–14, Romans 12:6–8, 1 Peter 4:10–11, and Ephesians 4:8–11. In these passages more than thirty different spiritual gifts are listed. I do not believe that the lists are intended to be exhaustive. Since there are several different lists, and they are all different, they are obviously intended to be only illustrative. If they were intended to be an exhaustive list, then they would all contain the same gifts.

For the sake of clarity let's divide these gifts into three divisions for discussion. They are the spectacular gifts, the service gifts, and the speaking gifts. We cannot cover every gift mentioned in the Bible, but here are some that are representative.

The Spectacular Gifts

The spectacular gifts include gifts such as miracles, healing, tongues, and the interpretation of tongues. Naturally these gifts create the greatest amount of interest and speculation. They are also the objects of great controversy and disagreement. There are some people who believe that these gifts were given only temporarily in order to authenticate the gospel message in the New Testament world. They believe that they passed away or became outdated with the apostles and that these gifts are no longer operative today.

There are others who believe just as strongly that these gifts are as valid today as they were in the first century. Whatever your position may be, you certainly must agree that the gifts should be used in accordance with God's original purpose. They should be used to help build up the body of Christ for the common good of all. And they should be used to create unity in his fellowship. Unless they are used to serve and to magnify the Lord and to forward his kingdom, they are being perverted.

The most intriguing of the spectacular gifts is that of tongues (1 Cor. 12:10). This has reference to ecstatic and unintelligible utterances which could not be understood without the aid of an inspired interpreter. The apostle Paul dealt with this subject in 1 Corinthians 12–14. The apostle Paul did not deny that speaking in tongues was a gift of the Holy Spirit, but he did minimize it.

The Corinthians were making it a mark of a super saint. So Paul wrote these words to put tongues in their proper perspective. He put first one limitation and then another around the gift of speaking in tongues. Eventually he had it so fenced in that there was little possibility of a person's using it except in private devotion. I believe that the use of tongues, if they are used at all, should be as a prayer language to God. Paul made it clear that they should not be used in public services unless an interpreter is present. Even then no more than three people should speak in tongues in a service. And women should not speak in tongues at all (1 Cor. 14:27–28,34).

Along with the gift of tongues was also the gift of interpretation (1 Cor. 12:10). Since a person was not to speak in tongues unless an interpreter was present, these two must go hand in hand. Someone must be able to explain in intelligible language what the tongue speaker was saying. I can understand how in the days before the New Testament was formed there may have been a need to get a firsthand message from God. However, in our day the Word of God has been given through the inspiration of the Holy Spirit and written down for our instruction. So I see little use in that kind of direct inspirational utterance. What message could they bring that God hasn't already spoken?

Another spectacular gift is the gift of healing (1 Cor. 12:9). You may ask, "Do you believe in divine healing?" I certainly do! Emphatically so. There are so many evidences around us that I cannot help it. But I do not believe in divine healers. I do not believe in the professional who travels around the country, rents an auditorium or a tent, and makes a living by pretending to heal the sick. Most of them are itinerants. Their life and work cannot stand the test of time and investigation. Therefore, they have to stay on the move.

But I still believe that people can be healed in miraculous ways. Jesus healed people. He did it because of his love for them. And he commanded his disciples to heal also. And they went out in the name of Jesus and healed. They were not always successful, by the way. No healer will be. The apostle Paul raised people from the dead, but he could not heal Timothy. Timothy had stomach problems, and Paul wasn't able to help him and so he recommended the best medicine of his day (1 Tim. 5:23).

The apostle Paul practiced divine healing, but he also believed in using the best medicine possible. There are some people who have the gift of praying for the sick and their prayers seem to have an unusual effect. James says, "Is any sick among you? let him call for the elders of the church; and let them pray over him, anointing him with oil in the name of the Lord: And the prayer of faith shall save the sick" (Jas. 5:14–15). This is a ministry that we have neglected in our churches today.

Another spectacular gift is the gift of miracles (1 Cor.

12:10). The word "miracles" means "powers." It may have to do with the power of exorcism, the power to dispel demons. Jesus cast demons out of people. The apostles cast demons out of people. And I have talked with some of our missionaries who say they have cast demons out of people. Demons are real and Satan is real, but God is greater than both and he is able to deliver people from their domination. Therefore, it is altogether possible that there are people who have a gift of miracles or the power to cast out demons.

The Service Gifts

These gifts quietly manifest themselves in the church by serving and ministering to other people. They include things such as faith, wisdom, knowledge, discerning spirits, ministry, administration, benevolence, and consolation. These gifts do not have the glitter and glamour of the first group, but they are far more important (1 Cor. 12:22–25).

The church can go a long while without tongues or their interpretation, without miraculous healings, and without exorcism. But let it try to exist without mercy, contributions, or teachings and you will see how important these gifts are.

The gift of ministry (Rom. 12:7) or helps (1 Cor. 12:28) is the gift of practical service. It ranks high on the list of the gifts of the Holy Spirit. It involves almost any work of practical service and social ministry to the needy. There are many people who can never speak to thousands. Many could never sway an audience. But they can minis-

ter in the name of Jesus Christ through doing simple
things like helping the poor or visiting the hospitals.
They are like Dorcas, who sewed clothes and gave them
to the poor and needy (Acts 9:36).

The gift of consolation is a special ability to offer comfort to the sorrowing or distressed (Rom. 12:8).
Onesiphorus must have had this gift. Paul said, "He
often refreshed me" (2 Tim. 1:16–18). The word "refreshed" suggests that he was like a breath of fresh air,
and he braced Paul up every time he went to visit him.
There are some people who can walk into a hospital room
and they are like a sunbeam bursting through the window. There is new joy and happiness because of their
presence.

The gift of ruling (Rom. 12:8) or governments (1 Cor.
12:8) is the gift of leadership. The word "ruleth" means
"he who is placed in front." It refers to anyone placed in
a position of authority. It is the gift of administration. It
is the ability to organize people and get things done.
There are some people who can do that and some who
can't. There are some who appear to be born leaders and
some who appear to be born followers. It is good to know
which you are. And if God has given you the ability to
organize and get things done, then you ought to use it in
his service.

Maybe you aren't effective at visiting people in the
hospital, but you could organize a hospital visitation
program and see that others do it. That's just as much a
gift from the Spirit as the gift of ministering. If that is
your gift, Paul said you should put some zip into it.

The gift of giving is another service gift (Rom. 12:8). The word "giveth" means "to impart" or "to share with." The Bible suggests that God has given some people the ability to give simply and without a great deal of fanfare. This I believe also implies the ability to make money. Everything some people touch turns to money. Everything some of us touch turns to red ink. If God gives you the ability to make money, he gives it to you for the purpose of giving that money away. He does not give it to you so you can hoard it up for yourself and build an empire and live like a king. He gives it to you so you can use it in the kingdom of God. What a difference there would be in God's work if there were more men like Barnabas who gave so generously. We would have more than we need to do God's work. If you have the ability to make money, you are not a self-made man. Your success is not due solely to your skill, wisdom, or hard work. God gave you the ability and you should return the fruit of it to him joyfully and freely.

The gift of faith is the ability to believe God to an unusual degree (1 Cor. 12:9). We all have some faith or we are not Christians (Eph. 2:8–9). This faith is a special kind. It is miracle-believing faith. It is the kind of faith that believes that God can do anything. What's more, it believes that God will. Some people have this unusual ability to believe God. Such people ought to give themselves continually to prayer.

A preacher named George Muller was a man like this. He lived such an unusual life of faith that his life was filled with miracle after miracle.

One day he was to sail on a ship, but a heavy fog came in so that the ship couldn't sail. He went to the captain and said, "Captain, let's pray about the matter." The captain was an infidel and wasn't interested in praying, but to pacify the preacher he agreed. They got down on their knees and George Muller in his simple, childlike way just said, "God, I want you to take away the fog. I want you to lift it so that we can sail and I can go on my mission." When he was finished with his childlike prayer, he said "Amen," and got off his knees. He said, "Captain, there is no need for you to pray." And the captain asked, "Why?" He replied, "For two reasons. One is that you are an infidel; you don't believe. And the second is, it's already happened." And they looked outside and the fog was gone. There are some people who have that kind of faith. It is a gift from God.

The gift of wisdom and knowledge seem to go together (1 Cor. 12:8). Wisdom means "insight" and knowledge means "application." It is the ability to mine spiritual truths from God's Word and systematize them so that others can use them. It is the ability to apply the principles of Scripture as Solomon did (1 Kings 3:16–28). The Holy Spirit gives to some people unusual insight to see into the heart of a problem or into the truth of God. He gives others the unusual ability to apply these insights and truths to practical everyday living. This is not common sense. It is uncommon sense. It is unusual insight and unusual knowledge. It is the ability to apply the insights and the wisdom in practical down-to-earth ways. These gifts can be invaluable to teachers, counselors, preachers, and leaders alike.

The gift of discernment is a gift of protection (1 Cor. 12:10). It is insight to tell truth from error. It is the gift Peter exercised when he knew Ananias had lied (Acts 5:3). How we need this today. John writes, "Beloved, believe not every spirit, but try the spirits whether they are of God: because many false prophets are gone out into the world" (1 John 4:1). We are not to believe everything that is said in the name of religion. We are not to believe every preacher on the radio or television. There are many false preachers in the world today. God gives some people the ability to know when a man is of God or when he is not. We need this ability and gift today.

The Speaking Gifts

These are gifts that have to do with the public ministry to the body of Christ. In these gifts prophecy is always first. It is the most important of the spiritual gifts. Not all gifts are of equal value. Paul says, "Greater is he that prophesieth than he that speaketh with tongues" (1 Cor. 14:5). The word "prophecy" means "inspired preaching." It is the only gift that Paul mentions every time he lists the gifts of the spirit. In four places he lists the gift of prophecy and it is the only gift he lists every time. It is the ability to announce the message of God convincingly. If a man has this ability, it is a gift from God. It came by grace.

No man is a born preacher. Nor is he a self-made preacher. The gift of teaching is the ability to explain and apply the Word of God so that the average person can understand it (Rom. 12:7). The Word of God needs not only to be proclaimed. It needs to be explained. To be able to open the Word of God and set it forth clearly is a most important gift.

The gift of exhortation is the ability to encourage and inspire people to give their lives to Christ (1 Cor. 12:8). Years ago churches had what they called exhorters. These were people who were called upon after the preaching and teaching to encourage and exhort people to give their lives to Christ. One man would preach the message and the exhorter would then appeal to them to give their lives and hearts to the Savior. Real preaching ought to include not only announcing the message of Christ, but exhorting people to respond to it and to receive him as their Savior.

These then are samples of the spiritual gifts. You should seek with all of your heart to discover, develop, and dedicate your gift to God. You ask, "How can I know my spiritual gift?" These things might help you.

(1) Acquaint yourself with the scriptural description of gifts.

(2) Know yourself. We don't get far in life until we know ourselves pretty well. An honest, prayerful assessment of your abilities without conceit or false modesty will help. Consider your likes and your dislikes. Give yourself time to experiment and become aware of the gifts and abilities that are yours.

(3) Consult others. Ask them to help you. They often see your gift before you do.

(4) Pray. Ask God for leadership and guidance in knowing how you are best suited to serve him.

The tremendous implication of all this is that when you were saved, the Holy Spirit gave you a gift, an endowment, an ability to work in the kingdom of God. And you ought to discover that gift and begin to put it to use. When that happens the church ceases to be preacher-centered. It becomes people-centered and the work of God goes on in a greater way.

Someone has said that the power of God does not come upon a program, but upon people. God's gifts do not come upon a program, but upon people. We need to make ourselves available to it, to be used of him to do whatever he wants us to do.

Years ago there was a train wreck and people were injured, wounded, and dying everywhere and there was a doctor on the train. Someone rushed up to him and said, "Doctor, doctor, why don't you do something? Help these people." And he said, "I can't do much because I didn't bring my instruments with me." Sometimes the hands of the Great Physician are tied because his instruments those people anointed and endowed, and equipped to do his work are not available for his service.

7
Serving—Little Things, Little People, and Little Thought

In a small town where I once pastored, a man's home caught fire one Sunday morning about church time. The little community had only a volunteer fire department. So the call came to all four churches in town for men to help fight the fire. Three of the churches quickly dismissed their services to help the neighbor save his home. But when one of the ministers was informed of the need, he refused. He said, "We will not dismiss our services. We are not going to let anything interfere with our worship of God." So while he and his people went through the forms of worship, their neighbor's house burned down.

There is something wrong with a religion that can sit idly by while a neighbor calls "Come help me fight fire." There must be a time for worship in the Christian's life. We all agree to that. But there must also be a time for fighting fires.

Worship and service are both vital parts of the Christian's life. The two are not in conflict but are complementary to one another. To follow Christ demands that we keep a good balance between the two.

Jesus spotlighted the means of service to God when he

painted a verbal picture of the judgment day. He said that when all nations stand before him, he will divide them into two groups. He will divide them as a shepherd divides his sheep from his goats. The sheep will be on his right hand and the goats on his left. Then he will commend and reward the sheep according to their deeds. Some have fed the hungry, clothed the naked, and visited the sick. Others have befriended the lonely and encouraged the wayward.

Then they will express their amazement at his commendation, asking when they had done these things. He will reply "Inasmuch as ye have done it unto one of the least of these my brethren, ye have done it unto me" (Matt. 25:40). Then he'll reprove and announce judgment to those on his left hand (the goats) for failing to do these very same things. They too shall express their amazement, asking when they had failed to minister unto him. He shall reply, "Inasmuch as ye did it not to one of the least of these, ye did it not to me" (Matt. 25:45).

The significance of this passage is that it tells us how we can serve God. We serve him by helping our fellow man. God sees what we do for others as service rendered to himself. We worship God by prayer, Bible study, singing, and going to church. We serve God by ministering to human need in everyday life. All are important. All have a place in the Christian life. We can never be content just to sing and pray and study our Bibles. We must serve God also. And we serve him by helping others.

Matthew 25:31–46 tells us three things that are important in serving God.

In Serving God, Little Things Are Important

When Jesus talked about service, he spoke of doing the simplest things for people. He talked about feeding the hungry, clothing the poor, and befriending the lonely. He talked of visiting the sick and ministering to the imprisoned. These are little things that each of us can do. There is nothing dramatic or spectacular about them. They are little things, but they are important. It may be that we miss real opportunities to serve God because we're overlooking the little things.

George Washington Carver was a great Negro scientist who discovered over three hundred uses for the peanut. Thus he greatly increased the potential of southern agriculture and he helped all people. Once in a speech he told the story of his single most crucial undertaking. While groping for solace one October day, he had walked through the predawn darkness of his beloved woodlands. He searched for the first glimmer of the new morning. Then, he had cried out, "Oh, Mr. Creator, why did you make this universe?

"And the Creator answered me, 'You want to know too much for that little mind of yours.' He said, 'Ask me something more your size.'

"So I said, 'Dear Mr. Creator, tell me what man was made for.'

"Again he spoke to me: 'Little man, you are still asking for more than you can handle. Cut down the extent of your request and improve the intent.'

"And then I asked my last question. 'Mr. Creator, why did you make the peanut?'

" 'That's better!' the Lord said, and he gave me a handful of peanuts and went with me back to the laboratory and together we got down to work."

Are you like that? Are you so busy looking for a cosmic-sized task that you overlook the peanut-sized opportunity right at hand? All around us are little things that need to be done for other people. They are things all of us can do. And if we do them, God considers them as acts of service to himself. The value of your good works is not based on their number, nor on their excellence. The value is on the love of God which prompts you to do them. In serving God, little things are important.

In Serving God, Little People Are Important

Concerning service, Jesus said, "Inasmuch as you have done it unto one of the least of these my brethren, you have done it unto me." Note the word "least." It means those least in the estimation of men. It refers to those who are considered by others as little or unimportant people. All of us consider some people big and some people little. And most people are anxious to serve those who are considered "big." The important people often have so many people around them that they get in the way of each other. But the "least," those who are little in the estimation of men, are often overlooked. Jesus says they also are important.

How do you measure a man? What standard do you

use? Do you measure him by the color of his skin? By his wealth? By his education? Most people are considered "big" or "little" on the basis of such superficial measurements. But every soul has value in God's eyes. He loves all men. He takes no such measurements. There are no "little" people in his sight.

The fact that man was created in the image of God gives value to every person. Don't ever forget that this worth and dignity applies to man as man. It is just as true of the man living on one side of the tracks as on the other. It applies to the man living in the river bottoms as well as the one living in the big house on the hill. It is as true of the man living in slums as it is of the man living in the best residential area of the city. The fact that Christ died for all men also confirms it. With him all of our man-made distinctions are erased.

When you are tempted to think of some men as being little, remember that great men stand on the shoulders of little men. How could we read Shakespeare without the printer and the binder? Maybe the little people are more important than we have thought.

Since God cares for all men, even those who are least in the estimation of men, whatever we do for others is counted as service to himself. When we do little things for little people, it is the same as doing it for Christ.

In Serving God, Little Thought of Reward Is Important

Christ rebuked the wicked for failing to meet human need. They asked, "When saw we thee an hungred . . . and did not minister unto thee?" (Matt. 25:44). It was as if they were saying, "If we had only known it was you, Lord, we would have helped." We can understand how the wicked would try to justify their failure to do good by pleading ignorance. The amazing thing is that when the righteous were commended for their goodness, they made the same response. They said, "When saw we thee an hungred, and fed thee?" (Matt. 25:37). The righteous were as unconscious of their goodness as the wicked were of their neglect.

Doing evil can become a habit. But so can doing good. Our goodness is to be so natural and so spontaneous that we do it without being aware of it. We are to do it with little or no thought of reward and recognition. The more Christlike we become the more natural and spontaneous our goodness will become.

A faithful servant of God once gave an example of this kind of service. She told of visiting an eighty-nine-year-old lady in a rest home one Sunday afternoon. As she handed her a little gift, the lady looked up from her bed. She smiled and said, "Thank you. I'll do something for you some day." The visitor told her she already had.

Then the visitor reminded her that years before she and her invalid husband had lived across the street from the church that the little old lady attended regularly. Each Sunday morning she had left some delicious contribution toward their Sunday dinner. She reminded her especially of the fried apple pies she had often left.

Then the little old lady said, "I'd forgotten about that." And the friend replied, "That's what Jesus wanted you to do."

My mind has clung to the experience since I heard it, and this thought is the result—for a gift to be a gift the giver must let go of it.

We are to do good and let God keep the records. We are to help people and not worry about rewards or recognition or praise. Our goodness is to be so natural and spontaneous that we do it without thinking about getting credit for it. God promises not to forget our acts of kindness even if we do (Heb. 6:10).

Martin of Tours was a Roman soldier and a Christian. One cold winter day, as he was entering a city, a beggar stopped him and asked him for alms. Martin had no money, but the beggar was blue and shivering with cold. So Martin gave him what he had. He took off his soldier's coat, worn and frayed as it was. He cut it in two and gave half of it to the beggar. That night he had a dream. In it he saw the heavenly places and all the angels and Jesus in the midst of them. He saw Jesus wearing half of a Roman soldier's cloak. One of the angels said to him, "Master, why are you wearing that battered old cloak? Who gave it to you?" And Jesus answered softly, "My servant Martin gave it to me."

A Christian is a servant. If you are to serve him in a pleasing and acceptable way, you must do little things for little people with little thought of reward. That's the kind of service God wants. I hope you'll begin giving it at your next opportunity.

8
Loving—Lifting the Fallen

Henry Ward Beecher once said, "The church is not an art gallery for the display of eminent saints, but a hospital for the curing of weak ones." How I wish the world had this concept of the church today. There is nothing more misunderstood than the church. Most people believe the church is a place for good people to go.

Often, because they know they are not good, they refuse to attend for fear of being hypocritical. Others feel they are just as good morally as those who attend regularly so they conclude they do not need to go. There are still others who believe that since they go regularly, they are superior to other people.

We need to see the church as a hospital to help the needy. The church is not a place for good people to go. The church is a place for sinners. So if you are a sinner and know it, then you ought to feel right at home in church. The church is nothing but a congregation of sinners who have been saved by the grace of God. They are seeking, by the power of Jesus Christ, to become what they ought to be.

We Christians make no claim to self-righteousness. There is every sin you can imagine in our hearts and

lives. We are sinners and know it. We are not what we
ought to be and we regret it. This is what takes us back
Sunday after Sunday to the house of God. We are there
for help.

The idea of the church as a hospital is scriptural. Paul
expresses this concept of the church when he writes,
"Brethren, if a man be overtaken in a fault, ye which are
spiritual, restore such an one in the spirit of meekness;
considering thyself, lest thou also be tempted" (Gal. 6:1).
There are several truths in this verse that will help our
concept of the church. It speaks of (1) the danger we all
face, (2) the duty we all have and (3) the disposition we
all need.

The Danger We All Face

A great danger faces every believer. It is expressed in
two words. The first is the word "fault." It is a strong
word for sin. It means a stark, staring, grievous sin. The
second is the word "overtaken." The verb "overtake"
means to slip accidentally, as a man may slip on an icy
road. Paul is saying that as we travel life's road we might
accidentally slip and fall into a grievous sin. He is saying
that life's pathway is strewn with banana peelings put
there by the devil. Any man, indeed every man, is in
constant danger of slipping and falling into a serious sin.
This is not an effort to minimize the seriousness of sin.
There is too much of that already. People try to minimize
the importance or the seriousness of sin in several ways
today.

First, they try to minimize sin by changing its name.

In a Rotary Club meeting several years ago, the speaker was trying to convince us to vote for a certain bond issue. The bond issue in part included a program for recycling and reusing "waste water." The speaker defined "waste water" as sewage water. But he said in trying to sell the program to the people, if you tell them that you are going to recycle or reuse sewage water, they don't like it, so he said, "We have found it is much more acceptable to use the word 'waste water' instead of the word 'sewage water!' " In either instance it is the same water. All you have changed is the name and one name seems more acceptable than the other.

People are that way about sin. An English minister, W. E. Sangster, told about attending a meeting of doctors, psychiatrists, and ministers who were discussing ways they could work together. Continually in the meeting they discussed the matter of premarital sex and extramarital sex and Sangster said that he clearly understood the meaning of those words. But, he said, there was an old country preacher who had trouble keeping his feet in the conversation. And so, somewhere in the middle of one of those discussions he stood up and said, "Premarital sex, extramarital sex? Are you talking about fornication and adultery?" And Sangster said, "I can still see the astonishment on the faces of all who were present at the use of those old-fashioned biblical words for sin."

We have a way nowadays of calling sin a mistake, or a social blunder, or an error, anything but what it really is. Billy Sunday said we would get along better if we treated sin like a rattlesnake instead of like a cream puff. One way we can deal with sin correctly is to call it by its right name.

Second, people try to minimize the seriousness of sin by blaming their circumstances. What about the man who gets involved with somebody else's wife? He explains it by saying, "I was lonely," or "My wife treated me coldly." What about the man who starts drinking too much? He explains it by saying, "Well, the pressures of life were too great." Or what about the man who begins to take money out of the till? He explains it by saying, "I had debts I couldn't pay," or "The boss wasn't paying me enough money anyway."

In every instance he is blaming his circumstances for his sin. He will not face up to the fact that there are other men who are lonely who don't commit immorality. There are other men who face the pressures of life who don't turn to artificial means of escape. There are other people who are underpaid and have more bills than they can take care of who don't turn to stealing. He fails to admit that he simply does not have the moral strength to stand up and do what is right. His problem is not his circumstances; his problem is his character.

Others minimize the seriousness of sin by claiming that these old sins are out-of-date. They call the moral code of the Ten Commandments Victorian or something like that. But God's moral standards are timeless. They endure forever. God did not simply give the Ten Commandments to Moses and to the Israelite nation. God gave the commandments through Moses to all men for all time. So when Paul uses the words "fault" and "overtaken," he is not trying to minimize the seriousness of sin. He is recognizing the weakness of human flesh. He is acknowledging the fact that there are frailties and susceptibilities in the life of every man. All of us, as we walk life's way, are in danger of slipping and falling into a serious sin.

The Duty We All Have

What then is our duty to a brother who falls into sin? Paul says, "Ye which are spiritual, restore such an one in the spirit of meekness; considering thyself, lest thou also be tempted."

When we travel down life's road and we see a brother down and out, what is our duty? There are three options open to us. We can ignore him, deplore him, or restore him.

First, we can ignore the brother. That is what most people do. They are traveling down life's road. They see a brother who is down and out and they just pass by on the other side. They justify their indifference by saying, "It's none of my business." But it is our business. Paul makes that very clear.

I have always considered it my business as a Christian minister to help a brother who is down and out. I have tried to practice that in the years I have been preaching. Say I learn that some man in my congregation is running around with another man's wife. I don't wait until the man yells for help or until his own wife comes crying for help. I go to him and try to set him on his feet again. You say, "But, preacher, that's not any of your business." In one sense of the word you are right. But it's God's business and I work for God. Paul is saying that it is not only the responsibility of the minister. It is the responsibility of every believer to help a man who is down and out.

Second, we can deplore him. That means we can criticize, we can find fault with him, and we can throw stones at him. I've heard it said that the Christian army is the only army in the world that shoots its wounded. Often as we travel down life's road we see a brother down and out and we just shoot him down verbally. Instead of putting an arm around him and setting him on his feet again, we castigate him verbally for his mistake.

Many people in the church today are precise and correct morally but cold and indifferent to the needs of others. They are good men. But you could not go to them and pour out your heart full of mistakes and failures and sins. You would receive no sympathy, no understanding, no encouragement from them. They are, as Mark Twain described them, good men in the worst sense of the word.

Third, we can restore him. The word "restore" is a medical term. It means to set in joint. It describes what a doctor does to a broken or dislocated bone. He sets it back in place. He puts the two pieces back into right relationship with one another. Paul says that is what we are to do as Christian brothers. When a man is down and out, don't ignore him, don't deplore him—restore him! Pick him up. Set him on his feet again. Put your arm around him and help him to get on his way in the

Christian life. This idea depicts for us the church of Jesus Christ as a hospital. It is in the business of curing weak brothers, of picking men up and of setting them on their feet again.

The Disposition We All Need

When we find a brother who has slipped and fallen into a serious sin, we are to set him on his feet again. We are to do this in meekness, considering ourselves, lest we also be tempted. Paul is saying that as you reach down to pick that brother up, let there be not a tinge of self-righteousness, pride, arrogance, or superiority in you. But in the spirit of love, tenderness, and meekness, reach down to help him, remembering all the while that you may be the next man down, or as Paul puts it, "considering thyself, lest thou also be tempted."

There is no room in our lives for arrogance, pride, or superiority. If we are wise, we will run a little bit scared, because we too can slip and fall. We need to face it. In each of us, there is the potential to commit every grievous sin you can imagine. Don't boast about what you would never do. There is the potential in your heart to do anything. Under the right set of circumstances, any of us might commit the very sin we most deplore in someone else.

Do you know the person I trust least of all in life? It's myself. I don't boast about what I'll never do. I just say, "By the grace of God, I don't want to do it," and I live my life running from the sins I may fall into. Paul tells us about that in 1 Corinthians 10:12. He said, "Wherefore let him that thinketh he standeth take heed lest he fall."

The next verse contains a marvelous promise, "There hath no temptation taken you but such as is common to man: but God is faithful, who will not suffer you to be tempted above that ye are able; but will with the temptation also make a way to escape, that ye may be able to bear it" (1 Cor. 10:13).

There is a marvelous promise for victory over temptation and sin. But, if we are proud or overconfident, then we might just nullify God's promise. He says, "So let every man who thinketh he standeth take heed lest he fall." The Bible says, "The heart is . . . desperately wicked: who can know it?" (Jer. 17:9). You can't know your own heart. I don't know my own heart. Only God knows the hearts of men. Because our hearts have such a potential for evil, we must never boast, never be proud, never act superior to someone else. And when we see a brother down and out, in meekness and in fear we must reach down to pick him up, and set him on his feet again.

In the Old Testament there is an interesting story that describes the perversity of the human heart. It involves King Ben-hadad of Syria. He was seriously ill and he heard that the prophet of God, Elisha, was in the territory. He knew that the prophet of God could foretell the future. So he decided to send word to the prophet to inquire about his health and his recovery. So he sent his trusted servant, Hazael, to ask Elisha if he would recover from the illness. Hazael found the prophet of God and inquired of him concerning the king's health. Elisha said, "The Lord has shown me that he will recover from his illness but that he shall die."

Elisha stood there gazing into the eyes of Hazael, and as he looked he began to weep. Being troubled by the tears Hazael said, "My master, why do you weep?" And Elisha said, "Because God has shown me the great evil that you shall do." He said, "God has shown me, Hazael, that you will tear down the strong places of Israel, that you will kill Israel's young men, that you will dash the children against rocks, that you will disembowel the women of Israel." And when he told Hazael that, Hazael said in astonishment, "Is thy servant a dog that he would do such a thing?" and he turned and stalked away in anger. He gave the report to his master, "The prophet of God said you will get well." And that night Ben-hadad, the king of Syria, slept in peace for the first time in many nights.

The next day, early in the morning, Hazael went into the king's bedroom. He took a wet towel and pressed it down over the face of his master and held it there tightly. There was a moment of struggle but soon it was over. The king had breathed his last breath and Hazael begin to reign as king of Syria. He went on to inaugurate a reign of terror such as had not been known before. He fulfilled every prophecy made by the man of God. You see, Hazael did not know the potential wickedness of his own heart. He did not know the evil that lurked there, and neither do we know the evil in our hearts.

Therefore, in the spirit of meekness and fear, let us seek to lift the fallen who on life's journey have slipped into grievous sin. As we do it, let us remember that we

too have been lifted by the grace of God. The song writer
says it so well:

> "In loving-kindness Jesus came
>   My soul in mercy to reclaim,
> And from the depths of sin and shame
>   Thro' grace He lifted me.
> From sinking sand He lifted me,
>   With tender hand He lifted me,
> From shades of night to plains of light,
>   O praise His name, He lifted me!"

Charles Gabriel

9
Contending—The Christian Manifesto

One of the most powerful pieces of literature ever written is the *Communist Manifesto*. It is a small pamphlet of about forty pages written in 1848 by Karl Marx and Fredrick Engels. It constitutes the party platform of the Communist party. In it Marx and Engels state what they believe and what they expect to happen in the world. Then it closes with a rousing call to arms.

Every believer needs a Christian manifesto. We need a clear, concise statement of what we believe. And we need a call to arms for Christians everywhere to unite in the cause of Christ. The reason we need a Christian manifesto is that the average Christian is about as well equipped to contend on fundamentals with an unbeliever as a boy with a peashooter is to facing a machine gun.

We do not know what we believe or why we believe it. The Scriptures agree. This truth is clearly set forth in the book of Jude. Jude said, "Beloved, when I gave all diligence to write unto you of the common salvation, it was needful for me to write unto you, and exhort you that ye should earnestly contend for the faith which was once delivered unto the saints" (Jude 3).

Jude tells us that he had intended to write a letter about salvation. But false teachers were at work in the church, so a doctrinal treatise was more needful. Thus, he decided to deal with the subject of apostasy. First, he urged us to contend earnestly for the faith which was once delivered unto the saints.

The word "faith" has reference to the whole scope of Christian doctrine without addition or deletion of that which was given to us by inspired writers.

Then he tells us that the faith was "once delivered." The word "once" means once and for all. It sets forth the idea of the final revelation that God has given to us in the person of Jesus Christ. This body of truth centers around him and it was given to us full and complete. You ask, "Should I believe what my grandfather believed?" Yes! For all the changes in society do not affect eternal truth at all. So the faith has been given to us once and for all.

Then Jude says that we should earnestly contend for this faith. We need more than familiarity and fondness for the faith; we need to be ready to fight for it. And we should earnestly contend, or strive, for the faith God has once and for all given to us.

Christians need to know what they believe. In the interest of defending the faith and the truth of Jesus Christ, I want to set forth for you my ideas of a Christian manifesto.

I Believe That Jesus Christ Is the Son of God and That He Is the Savior of All Who Believe in Him

Paschal said, "The last thing one settles in writing a

book is what one should put first." But when we begin to write a Christian manifesto there is no doubt as to what should be first. We begin with Jesus Christ, for the Christian faith is forever linked with the person of Jesus. We build our faith and our hope solidly upon him. Christianity is not just a code of ethics. It is not just a philosophy of life. It is not just a system of rituals and ceremonies. Christianity is basically and essentially a personal relationship with God through Jesus Christ. Everything hinges upon his identity and our relationship to him.

When Jesus was here in the flesh, he asked the question, "Whom do men say that I the Son of man am?" (Matt. 13:17). In the nineteen hundred years that have followed, over sixty thousand books have been written to answer that question.

There are those who say that Jesus Christ was only a myth, a figment of the ancient imagination. Some say that Jesus was only a man. They say that Jesus was a great moral teacher, that he has had a profound influence upon the world, but that there is nothing divine about him. But we Christians say that Jesus is not a myth and that he was and is more than just a man. He is in fact God. He is not just a part of God, or just sent by God, or just related to God. He was and is God. And thus he is the Savior of all who believe in him.

He was born of a virgin. He lived a sinless life. He taught as no man ever taught. He was able to make the blind see and the deaf hear and the lame walk. He was crucified on the cross, and he was raised from the dead on the third day. He showed himself alive with many invaluable proofs, and he ascended into heaven. Jesus Christ is alive today! The deep significance of his life, his death, and his resurrection is that he might bring us to God. Through Jesus the way of salvation and redemption has been provided for everyone.

I Believe That the Bible Is the Word of God

The Bible is the inspired, authoritative, all-sufficient food for my soul. If Jesus is the way, then the Bible is the road sign along the way to guide and direct me in the things of God.

A few months ago I bought a new automobile. With it came an operator's manual that told me about the various instruments on the dashboard, and told me how to operate and service my car for the greatest use. In exactly the same way, God has provided an operator's manual for my life. That manual is the Bible, the Word of God. It is inspired and authoritative and it teaches me what to believe and how to live. It is all-sufficient for my soul. Other books may be helpful, but no other book is necessary. The Bible is all that I need (2 Tim. 3:16–17).

It is not merely a collection of ancient writings. It is not simply the statement of an outdated moral code. It tells us of the mighty acts of God in the past. It gives the plan of God for the future. It is designed to tell lost people how to be saved and saved people how to live.

"But," someone will ask, "how can you possibly believe that an infinite God could put his whole wisdom into so small a book?"

I answer, "Who but God could do it?"

Listen, if Congress had written the Bible it would take a freight train to carry it. But since God did, I can carry it in my vest pocket. It is so full of wisdom that nineteen centuries of study by the world's best thinkers have been unable to exhaust it. Here is proof, demonstrable proof, that this book must have come from God. Of him alone can be said, "O the depth of the riches both of the wisdom and knowledge of God! how unsearchable are his judgments, and his ways past finding out!" (Rom. 11:33). There is no getting around that. I challenge any man on earth to answer that argument.

Ten thousand years from now, if people are still talking about God, they will be talking about him from the Bible. The language will be different perhaps, even as our language is different from that of the New Testament. But the book that God has given to us will continue to be a light to our path and the bread of God to feed our souls.

I Believe That the Holy Spirit Lives Within Me and Is My Helper for Life

The Christian life is no self-effort life. It is a life lived in the power of God's Spirit. Jesus promised the Holy Spirit to us. He said that he would pray to the Father and ask that he send another Comforter to abide with us forever (John 14:16). The word "comforter" means a road companion, someone to walk by one's side. He was saying that the Holy Spirit would be to all disciples in the future what he had been to them in the days of his flesh

(John 14:16–18).

On the day of Pentecost the Holy Spirit came in a special way. He is Christ's replacement and remains with us as a comforter and a helper. The Holy Spirit is our power for victorious living. He is the same Spirit that brooded over the chaotic mass in creation and transformed it into water. He is the same Spirit that endowed Solomon with universal wisdom. He is the same Spirit that came upon David and made him a man after God's own heart. He is the same Holy Spirit that raised Jesus from the dead. The Holy Spirit who came in those days with such unusual power can come into our hearts and lives even today.

So Christianity is not lived by self-effort alone. When we receive salvation we don't get a do-it-yourself kit. We don't come to Jesus by faith then go out and try hard to live the Christian life. The Christian life is a supernatural life made possible by the indwelling Spirit of God.

I Believe That the Church Is God's Means of Global Evangelism

Christians are people with a mission. Our mission is clear. It is to win all men everywhere to faith in Jesus Christ. The means of achieving this mission is the church. There is no doubt that God wants all people everywhere to be saved. He is "Not willing that any should perish, but that all should come to repentance" (2 Peter 3:9). There is no person outside his love and concern. His invitation is to all.

He says, "Whosoever will, let him take the water of

life freely" (Rev. 22:17). So it is God's desire that all men everywhere be saved.

More than that, in the Great Commission, he told us to go into all the world and preach the gospel (Matt. 28:19–20). God's means for global evangelism is the church. There is no need for any church anywhere to sit around wondering, "What should we do? What is our responsibility?" The true church is an outpost of the kingdom of God placed in a particular spot in the world to bear witness of the lordship of Jesus Christ.

A church is a mission living by the power of God in a world that sometimes hates it. The world is sometimes indifferent, and sometimes seeks to take the church captive. Any church that does not recognize the basic purpose of its existence is in jeopardy. To us has been given the high and the holy calling of sharing the good news of Jesus Christ with all men everywhere. The church has many critics, but it has few competitors in the field of global evangelism.

I Believe That the Return of Christ Is the Only Hope for Our World

We cannot look at our world today without feeling a bit of pessimism about it. We see war, poverty, hunger, disease, and racial strife everywhere we turn. Men, since the beginning of time, have looked at our world with all of its problems, and they have dreamed of a better day. They have dreamed of a utopia when men would study war no more, when death and disease would be conquered, and when the world of our dreams would become a reality. But this will never be until Jesus Christ comes back to earth again.

The hope of utopia is not in economics, as the Communists say. It is not in education or politics, as the humanists say. It is rather in the return of Christ, as the Bible says. The sinfulness of man prevents us from ever achieving utopia in this life.

Have you ever seen a chart that plots the moral progress of mankind? Your answer is obviously no, because there is no such graph, for there has been no such progress since the beginning of time. Technically, educationally, and athletically, man has advanced almost beyond the wildest dreams. But morally and spiritually he is still the same. This truth was impressed upon me by Paul Bellington, missionary to Brazil. He was asked if there was really any difference between primitive man and modern man. He related that in the area along the Amazon River where he works, there are eight uncivilized tribes that still live in a pre-Stone Age culture. They don't even have rocks and flints for their arrowheads. They use sharpened bamboo sticks. One of the tribes is even cannibalistic.

He said that while God has not called him to work among those tribes, he still tries to find out all he can about them. He told of meeting a government Indian agent one day and asking him, "Do the Indians fight much among themselves?" He replied, "Yes, they fight all the time." So Paul asked him what they fought about. The agent said, "They fight mostly about three things. First, they fight over property, a little piece of land or a bow and arrow, or a piece of monkey meat. Second, they fight over women. They don't marry. But they do pair off and live together. If one man starts looking at another man's wife, they fight over her. Third, they fight as a result of getting drunk. They make alcohol out of fermented fruit. They get drunk and then fight and kill one another."

Bellington said when he returned to his home a back issue of *Time* magazine had arrived in the mail. To his amazement it contained the results of a study by a Harvard professor dealing with violence in America. The professor analyzed its cause. He listed three principal reasons for violence. He said that men fight and kill over property, over women, and as a result of getting drunk.

There in stark similarity stood Stone Age man and Atomic Age man. They were really just alike morally.

Such illustrations are enough to make the most optimistic man pessimistic. There seems to be no hope for the world. But the Bible comes to us with the message of hope. It says, "Nevertheless we, according to his promise, look for new heavens and a new earth, wherein dwelleth righteousness" (2 Peter 3:13). Peter tells us that God has promised us a new heaven and a new earth where everything will be right.

A social worker goes into the slums to work with the poor. He is dreaming of a world where there will be no poverty. A scientist goes into the laboratory to find a cure for cancer. He is dreaming of a world where there will be no disease. A statesman sits down at the conference table to try to negotiate peace. He is dreaming of a world where there will be no war. But this will not become a reality until Jesus Christ comes back and there is a new heaven and a new earth.

In that world men "Shall beat their swords into plow-shares, and their spears into pruninghooks: nation shall not lift up sword against nation, neither shall they learn war any more" (Isa. 2:4). In those days the lamb shall lie down with the lion and we shall know peace and joy such as we have never known before.

History is ultimately Jesus' story. And we shall know peace when Jesus Christ reigns as Lord and Master over this universe.

Where is history headed? Amidst the world's confusion, God in his omnipotence is working out his everlasting plan and purpose. God is still in control, and God shall win the ultimate victory.

I Believe That People Will Spend Eternity Either in Heaven or in Hell

Jesus said, "Enter ye in at the strait gate: for wide is the gate, and broad is the way, that leadeth to destruction, and many there be which go in thereat: Because strait is the gate, and narrow is the way, which leadeth unto life, and few there be that find it" (Matt. 7:13–14).

There are two roads in life and two destinies from which a man has to choose. Christ does not divide men by the color of their skin or their economic condition or their educational achievements. Rather, he divides them into two classes. There are those who are on the broad road that leads to destruction. And there are those who are on the narrow road that leads to eternal life. The Bible says, "And as it is appointed unto men once to die, but after this the judgment" (Heb. 9:27). People are going to face God in eternity, and they shall spend that eternity either in hell or in heaven.

Winston Churchill said a few years ago that the moral landslide in Great Britain could be traced to the fact that heaven and hell were no longer proclaimed throughout the land. Someone has said that hell is getting very out-of-date in today's thinking. But it is not out of business! People are still going there.

There is also a heaven that God has prepared for us. It is a place where we shall have personal identity. We shall engage in purposeful service for the Lord. He has provided a heaven for us if we will believe and trust in Christ and accept him as our Savior.

Heaven is a literal place. It is the most beautiful place that the mind of God could conceive and the hand of God could create. It is a place where the mysteries of life shall be cleared up. It is a place where righteousness shall prevail. And God has made it possible for you to go there through Jesus Christ his Son.

Every Christian needs this manifesto. I commend it to you. Be familiar with it. Live by it. Be willing to fight for it.

And you will live and die a better Christian.

10
Witnessing—Your Faith: Contagious or Contaminated?

Two of my friends attended a Christian conference in California several years ago. The wife came back excited about some good things that happened there. One was that for the first time her husband realized it was his responsibility, not just the preacher's, to witness and share his faith. She hastened to say, "He's not doing it yet, but at least now he knows it is his responsibility."

A lot of Christians do not yet know that it is their responsibility to bear witness to their faith. Even more know it, but are not yet doing it. Sharing your faith with others is not only a mark of Christian maturity, but also a means of developing Christian maturity.

Witnessing is the responsibility of every Christian. Jesus said, "But ye shall receive power, after that the Holy Ghost is come upon you: and ye shall be witnesses unto me both in Jerusalem, and in all Judaea, and in Samaria, and unto the uttermost part of the earth" (Acts 1:8).

The word translated "witness" in the New Testament is both intriguing and revealing. It is the Greek word "martus." In general it refers to one who may be called upon to testify to an event at which he was present. A witness is one who is called upon to give credible evidence to an event about which he has personal knowledge. The Christian witness is commissioned to give a testimony regarding a personal experience. He is not one who speculates about what might happen when one believes in the Lord. He knows. He knows from personal experience.

It helps to remember what we are. We are not lawyers. We are not judges. We are not the jury. We are not the arresting officer. We are not the prosecuting attorney. We are witnesses. We are to share what we have come to know from our own personal experience. When we do this the Holy Spirit (the lawyer) uses our witness along with the witness of others to build a case in the life of the unbeliever. In time, hopefully, he will give his verdict in favor of Christ and become his follower.

The more we share our faith the stronger we grow spiritually. It is a rule of life that we become fully conscious only of what we are able to express to someone else. Knowledge remains vague as long as it is unformulated and unshared. Therefore, witnessing strengthens and matures us.

You may be thinking, "Man, that will be hard for me to do." Believe me, I understand. It's hard for me too. I don't like dogs nipping at my heels. I don't like rain dripping down my neck. I don't like skipping my favorite evening television program. However, I have no choice. My Master said go and all I can do is say, "Yes, Sir." L. R. Scarborough once said, "If a man is not witnessing for Christ he is guilty of high treason and spiritual re-

bellion." Besides that, the love of Christ constrains me
(2 Cor. 5:14). My concern for others causes me to go and
witness.

The failure to witness may very well be our greatest
failure today. We analyze, organize, and eulogize, but
we don't evangelize. Since this is our primary responsibility we must begin to witness for Christ as never before. As Chester H. Johnson said, "If your Christianity
isn't contagious, it must be contaminated." What's
necessary to a contagious faith? What is involved in the
right kind of witnessing and evangelism?

Evangelism Involves More People Than the Pastor

We must first remember that evangelism is every
Christian's job. R. A. Torrey, while conducting an
evangelistic crusade in Minneapolis years ago, asked a
man he had seen in the congregation several nights if he
were a Christian.

"I consider myself as such," was the somewhat dubi-
ous reply.

"Good," said Torrey, "are you bringing others to
Christ?"

With a bland smile the man said, "That's not my
business. I am a lawyer. It is your business to bring men
to Christ."

Quickly opening his Bible to the eighth chapter of
Acts, Torrey said, "Please read this," pointing to the
fourth verse.

The man read, "They that were scattered abroad went
everywhere preaching the word." "Ah, yes," said the

lawyer, "but they were apostles, ministers like yourself."

"I think you are mistaken, sir," answered Torrey. "Read this," and he pointed to the first verse: "They were all scattered abroad throughout the region of Judea and Samaria, except the apostles."

The call to be a Christian is a call to be a witness. In the Scriptures the word "witness" is used almost synonymously with the word "Christian." When a man is genuinely converted, he becomes a witness. That is his profession, his occupation, his life work. The desire to share what he knows of Christ becomes a motivating force in his life. He feels a heaviness of heart for the person who does not share his joy in Christ. He seeks opportunities to share his testimony with others.

This should be the spontaneous result of conversion. In the New Testament it was not urged, exhorted, and promoted. It just happened. The church did it without scolding, special meetings, or campaigns. It ought to be so today. It is safe to say that evangelism is inevitable in a spiritually robust life. Yet it has been strangely neglected by many Christians today. Someone has said, "We have raised up an army in which nobody fights but the generals." Howard Hendricks says, "The greatest threat to Christianity is not communism or atheism: it's Christians trying to get into heaven incognito without being involved or sharing their faith with others, or serving the Lord with their whole hearts."

Evangelism can never be left to a select few or to the spiritual elite. It is for all upon whom the Holy Spirit has come. It can never be optional for a layman. It is not a

game for those who like to play it, or for the unusually
devout. It is an obligation resting upon every member of
the body of Christ.

You ask, what then is the role of the pastor? It is not to
be the star player. He is more of a player-coach. He is to
train and equip laymen to do the work of the ministry
including evangelism. He participates himself while he
trains laymen (Eph. 4:11–12). We believe not only in the
priesthood of the believer; we believe also in the
"preacherhood" of the believer.

Evangelism Involves More Places Than the Church

Roy Fish, professor of evangelism at Southwestern
Baptist Theological Seminary in Fort Worth said, "We
must cease to think of the church as a place of
evangelism, and begin to think of it as the base of
evangelism." The church is to be a launching pad. It is to
be an equipping center. It is to be a filling station. And
we are to go out from it to witness to our world.

Getting out into the world where people are and sharing our faith with them is the only practical method of
winning our world to Christ. Churches often lament at
declining attendance by saying, "They won't come." And
the Lord must weep in heaven saying, "Yes, and you
won't go." Nowhere in the Bible are we told that the lost
are going to come to us. But repeatedly we are told that
we must go to them and share the good news of salvation. So we must get out of the church and go where
people are to witness effectively.

It is estimated that less than three percent of the lost

people ever come into our buildings. This will never reach our world. If great cathedrals would win the world, Europe would have won it long ago. If programs would win the world, Southern Baptists would have done it long ago. Jesus is our example. He met Peter at the docks, the woman of Samaria by the city waterworks, Matthew at the internal revenue office, and scores of others while they were in the process of their daily pursuits. He went to them. Few came seeking him. It was only after he sought men that they sought him.

We must get involved with people where they are. As in fishing, we must go where the fish are—to the best holes. We must go to bowling alleys, pizza parlors, drive-ins, golf courses, and every other place where people are and there make contact with them for Jesus Christ.

George H. Tolley tells of a Girl Scout leader who was once pulled up sharply by the remark of a young scout. She was a Roman Catholic and wore a religious medal which was hanging outside her uniform. The girl said, "Your religion is showing." Shouldn't it? Shouldn't it show in your office, shop, classrooms, politics, and in your own home? Robert Louis Stevenson said, "The cruelest lies are often told in silence." Perhaps when we should have spoken, we remained silent about redemption. This silence leads people to believe Christianity is not a truth but a fallacy. It leads them to believe it to be a half-truth at the best, and perhaps even a lie. It leads people to believe that Christ is not all he claims to be or we are not all we ought to be.

Evangelism Involves More Plans Than Preaching

Our task is to communicate the good news. How can we best do this? Preaching is one way. Paul says, "It pleased God by the foolishness of preaching to save them that believe" (1 Cor. 1:21). It is a very good way. It is an effective way, but it's not the only way. Perhaps our greatest heresy is that we have taken one way of evangelism and made it the only way to win people to Christ.

Living a good life is another way. Most people are won not by arguments, but by exposure. They need to see the power of Jesus Christ in your life. Peter tells us that we are to be ready always to give every man an answer for the hope that is in us. Then he adds, "Having a good conscience; that, whereas they speak evil of you, as of evildoers, they may be ashamed that falsely accuse your good conversation in Christ" (1 Pet. 3:16). Our testimony must be backed up and reinforced by a good life. I am not suggesting that you must be perfect. The world does not expect us to be perfect. It does expect us to be different. Satan wants to keep you quiet. One of his deceitful methods is to attempt to convince you that you mustn't witness to anyone about Jesus Christ until you are good enough to pass as Gabriel's twin. Unfortunately that time will never come.

Jesus told us to confess him before men. We confess him aright by life and by word. Our lives ought to speak louder than our words. But as a matter of fact they do not and perhaps cannot. As Sam Shoemake said, "I cannot, by being good, tell men of Jesus' atoning death and resurrection, nor of my faith in His divinity. The emphasis is too much for me and too little for him." Our lives must be made as consistent as we can make them with our faith. But our faith, if we are Christians, is vastly greater than our lives. That is why the word of witness is so important.

Few things are more effective than sharing your own personal experience. People can identify with it, there is an unusual amount of authority in it, and it can be used in many situations. Every Christian ought to take time to think through his own experience and then be able to express it in a believable, brief, and honest way. Your testimony should include parts of your past, present, and future.

You have not always been a Christian, so you ought to tell people something about your life before you became a believer. Be as honest and as true-to-life as possible. What was it like? How did you feel? Second, there was a time when you realized that you needed to become a Christian. How did that sense of need come? What caused you to turn to the Lord? Then there came a decisive act of commitment to Christ. When and where and how did that take place?

Finally, there has been a difference in your life since then. This is where your major emphasis should be. How is it now? What is there about it that someone else might want? Perhaps you have been more at peace with yourself, with God, and with your fellowman. Perhaps you have found new fulfillment in life. Perhaps you have developed a new love and appreciation for others. Perhaps you have found a whole new set of friends. Perhaps you have realized that there is a meaning to life beyond today. An honest, believable, clear sharing of these facts can be used of God to help others.

A basic knowledge of the Bible will be an additional help. Novelist Herman Wouk observed, "Some people think all the equipment you need to discuss religion is a mouth." We need a mouth, but we also need a mind. We need to know some things. We need to know that God loves us and has a marvelous plan for our life (John 3:16; 10:10). Secondly, we need to know that man is a sinner and separated from God (Eccl. 7:20; Rom. 3:23). We need to know that man is helpless to save himself by being religious or by being good (Eph. 2:8–9; Titus 3:5). Then we need to know that Christ is the one and only Savior (John 14:6; Acts 4:12). Finally, we need to know that men must receive Christ by personal invitation (Rom. 10:13; Rev. 3:20).

Be sensitive to people's needs. Man does not live by bread alone. People may live in lovely homes, drive big cars, be well dressed, and yet not be happy. Everybody has a problem or lives near one. Be sensitive to such needs. A man is oftentimes like an island. We must row around him several times before we find a place to put in. However, if we are patient and sensitive, we will soon discover that need and find an opportunity to share our faith and these gospel facts with him.

We must be bold, but not brazen. There is no place for rudeness in Christian witnessing. We are never to try to cram our faith down another person's throat. The great evangelist Dr. Turnbull was riding on a train next to a person who opened a flask and offered him a drink of whiskey. Dr. Turnbull declined the offer. A few minutes later the man repeated the offer, and again Dr. Turnbull turned him down. The third time the offer was made the man said to Dr. Turnbull, "I bet you think I am a rather evil man doing all this drinking, don't you."

"No," said Dr. Turnbull. "I was thinking what a generous man you are to keep offering me a drink." That entree was sufficient for Dr. Turnbull to lead the man to Christ before the journey ended.

Then pray and depend on the Holy Spirit to bless your witness. Jesus promised that the Holy Spirit would convict the world of sin, righteousness, and of the judgment to come (John 16:26–27). You do the witnessing and he will do the convicting.

Beyond this we need to use our imagination and get along. We can begin at home as Andrew did, and share our faith with our own family. We can use our social contacts as opportunities to share Christ. We can share Christian friends or our pastor by bringing them into contact with unbelievers in an informal situation. This gives them an opportunity to see that Christians are normal, fun-loving humans. This works wonders in breaking down barriers and developing friendships for future witnessing opportunities.

We can invite people to participate in Christian events such as church services, Bible studies, men's meetings, and the like. Many people who would never go on their own would attend such meetings at your invitation and as your guest. Letters or cards on special occasions that express concern and prayer can also be effective. Then we can always share good Christian literature and books with people at times of special need.

When Jesus called his first disciples he said, "Follow me and I will make you fishers of men" (Matt. 4:19). Are you following Christ in that sense? This is the world's greatest need and it is our greatest privilege.

Andrew Murray said, "There are two classes of people—soul winners and backsliders." Which will you be?

11
Giving—Life Principles of Stewardship

Beyond conversion there is a whole world of steward-ship that believers need to explore. "For God so loved the world, that he gave" (John 3:16). We are to so love the world and God that we give also. The Bible abounds with teachings to this end.

The most exhaustive statement of Christian steward-ship in the Bible is in 2 Corinthians, chapters 8 and 9. These two chapters are divided into three parts. The first part is a challenge to Christian giving through the exam-ple of the churches of Macedonia. Paul cites the example of those churches to inspire us to give. He tells how in spite of their deep poverty they gave liberally to the needs of others. They didn't wait to be asked. They actually begged for the opportunity to give. And when they gave, Paul said, they gave more than dollars and cents. They first gave themselves to the Lord (2 Cor. 8:1–9). So he holds them up as an eternal example to inspire us to Christian giving today.

The second division of this great teaching on steward-ship is an outline of Paul's plan for taking the collection. Paul was not only a good preacher and motivator, but also a good businessman. He recognized that he had his critics and there were those who would be quick to say, "Paul has an ulterior motive in what he is doing. He plans to take this money for his own personal needs." So Paul told them his plan. He told them he planned to send Titus and some other men who were highly respected and approved by the churches. They would oversee the collection and the administration of the money. Paul was setting out a great and an effective bookkeeping procedure so that whatever he did financially would be above reproach (2 Cor. 8:10–24).

The third division of this great teaching is a statement of the life principles of stewardship. I want to spotlight these principles in this chapter with the hope that you will be challenged to Christian stewardship and act on them in faith.

Let's look at them more closely so we can practice them more completely.

The Surest Way to Get Is to Give

If you want to have more, then you ought to give more. Paul says, "But this I say, He which soweth sparingly shall reap also sparingly; and he which soweth bountifully shall reap also bountifully" (2 Cor. 9:6). Paul is saying here that life is in many ways a boomerang. We get back as we give out. If we give more, then we shall get more. If we want to have more, then we need to learn to share more. He uses an illustration that is as common as life itself to present this great truth. He uses the illustration of a farmer who goes out in the springtime to plant seed. If he sows sparingly, then when the harvest time comes he shall gather sparingly. But if he sows the seed bountifully, then when the harvest day comes he shall gather in bountifully.

This is an unalterable principle of agriculture. If a farmer is stingy in his planting, when the harvest day comes, he is going to reap meager harvest. In fact, he is going to get back in direct proportion to the seed that he planted. So if he is wise in his agricultural methods, he will be liberal and generous at planting time.

That same principle of agriculture is a life principle of stewardship. You get as you give, so if you want to get a great deal back in your life, then you need to give a great deal. If you want to have more, then you need to give more. For a long time in my ministry, I shied away from teaching this. I'd always reasoned that if a man gives more because he gets more, then that would not be giving in the truest sense of the word. That would be trading. But as I have studied this passage of Scripture, I have come to the conclusion that this is exactly the way it is. The Bible does not avoid the idea that you get because you give and you have more because you share more.

God recognizes that it takes faith to believe and attempt even that. And it's faith God wants from us, not our money. I am persuaded that God would like for you to get in a giving contest with him. He wants you to begin giving to him so that he can return bountifully to you. If you would do that, you would discover the riches of God's resources. I am persuaded that the more you give the more you will get. This principle is true in all of life. Not just in fianances, but in every realm of life, the best way to get is to give.

Maybe you don't have very much energy. Maybe you are always tired. How can you get more energy? How do you get more strength and vitality for life if you are tired? Reason says the answer is to sit around all day and then go to bed early. Then keep doing that day after day. Keep all of your strength and all of your energy in you and you will get stronger and stronger. Isn't that the way it works? No! The opposite is true. If you want more energy, you use more energy. And if you want more strength and vitality, don't sit around in that easy chair all the time. Get on an exercise program. Start lifting weights or riding a bicycle or jogging. Expend some of your energy and energy will come back to you.

Joggers say of jogging, "Preacher, it makes you feel so good. It gives you strength and vitality all day." They expend energy and they get it back. One of the men in my church is going to run three thousand miles this year. He is so thin he looks like a zipper with his tongue hanging out. I tell him that when he dies he is going to be so healthy we are going to have to take a stick and beat his heart to death. People are going to walk by his casket and say, "That is the healthiest looking corpse I have ever seen in my life." Jogging makes him feel good.

Many of you are in an exercise program and you know that the best way to get energy is to give energy. Energy has a way of coming back to you. The same is true with forgiveness. Maybe you have had a disagreement with somebody and there is bitterness and strife between you. You would like to have forgiveness. What is the surest way of getting forgiveness? It is to give it. Go to that person and say "I forgive you and I want us to be reconciled." Give forgiveness and you discover amazingly and wonderfully that forgiveness comes back to you.

It is a principle of life that you get more when you give more, and if you want to have you need to share. The same thing is true with love. There are people all around us who feel that they are unloved. Nobody likes them. Nobody cares about them. If you want to be loved more, then start loving. Begin to express love and concern for some person in the finest and noblest sense of the word. You will discover that the more love you give, the more love you will receive. The Bible says, "A man that hath friends must shew himself friendly" (Prov. 18:24). That is a life principle. If we want friendship, we have to give friendship. Life works that way. It is like a boomerang. What we send out always comes back to us. It works in every area of life.

And I am persuaded this principle also works in the area of stewardship. That is exactly what God is saying here. If you give sparingly, you shall receive sparingly, and if you give generously, you shall receive generously. So, if you want to have more, start giving more. But, you say, this means that God is going to give you back more peace of mind, happiness, love, etc. That is right. But he is also saying that God is going to bless you in a material way.

If you don't believe me, then you try it. Begin to

practice it. Put God to the test. He tells us in the Bible that he is willing to be proved. In the book of Malachi he says, "Prove me now herewith, saith the LORD of hosts, if I will not open you the windows of heaven, and pour you out a blessing, that there shall not be room enough to receive it" (Mal. 3:10).

B. H. Carroll, past president of Southwestern Baptist Theological Seminary, once wrote to J. B. Gambrell, then state mission secretary in Texas, appealing for financial help for the seminary. Dr. Carroll ended his letter by saying, "Come down here and help me. I'm up a tree." Dr. Gambrell wrote expressing the reason that he was unable to give financial assistance. He ended it by saying, "I can't come and help you down out of the tree, because I'm in a hole." Dr. Carroll wrote back, "If you would come and help me down out of the tree, you would get out of the hole!"

You know what? Some of you are in a hole financially. And I am persuaded that you would get out of the hole if you would learn how to give more. Maybe the very reason that you are always in a financial bind is that you keep it all to yourself. You have never learned the principle of life that if you are going to have more, you need to give more. If you want to get, you need to share. God will help you get out of the hole if you will begin to help somebody who is up a tree. Until you have enough faith to believe and to try it, God can never bless you as he would like to.

That's why Paul says, "Every man according as he purposeth in his heart, so let him give; not grudgingly, or of necessity: for God loveth a cheerful giver" (2 Cor. 9:7). The word "cheerful" is from the Greek word that means hilarious. God loves a hilarious giver. If you are going to get as you give, then giving is not a drudgery nor a burden. Giving is an investment and it is a great joy. God is going to bless you in return. This is a principle of life. You get as you give. The surest way to have is to share.

You Need to Give According to God's Ability and Not Your Own

In this whole passage, Paul keeps emphasizing what God is able to do. He is not talking about what we are able to do. In fact, he says "God is able" (2 Cor. 9:8). And then he tells us what God is able to do. God can do all things. The word "able" means power, might, energy. That's what God has, power, might, and energy, to multiply everything we have.

And his power is all-encompassing. Five times in these verses he used the word "all" or "every." God can give you all things so that you may have everything that is necessary. He is talking about the bounty and the resources of God. After all, God owns everything. He owns the cattle on a thousand hills. "The earth is the LORD's and the fulness thereof" (Ps. 24:1). Our heavenly father is a rich man. He does not need anything. All the resources of this universe are at his disposal. God is able to multiply your possessions and to bless your life.

God can and will furnish the means of supplying all

needs. It's our responsibility to do right and then we shall have what we need. God will see to that. As Paul said, "But my God shall supply all you need according to his riches in glory" (Phil. 4:19).

So often when it comes to giving we look at our checkbook and our budget and our income. Then we say, "Oh, my, I am just not able to do that. I can't do that." But Paul is saying, "Listen, don't look at *your* ability. Look at *God's* ability. Ask what God can do." He is saying that God is able to make all grace abound for you that in all things you may abound to every good work.

Do not be afraid to impoverish yourself. God will supply your needs. What is God able to do? He tells us in Ephesians 3:20. It tells us that God is able to do everything we "ask." No, wait a minute, that's not enough. He is able to do everything we "ask" or "think." No, wait a minute, that's not enough. He is able to do "above" all that we ask or think. As if that weren't enough, he says that he is able to do "abundantly" above all that we ask or think. And finally he is able to do "exceeding" abundantly above all that we think or ask. That's what God can do and we are to give out of His abundance, not ours.

The Christian life in all of its aspects is to be an overflowing life. It is not to be a life of stinginess and inadequacy. It is to overflow from God's bounty. So do not hesitate to do what is right, and God will see to it that all of your needs are supplied. If you say, "I can't afford it," then you are not exercising any faith at all.

The More You Give the More You Will Have to Give

Then Paul tells us that God does not give to us to satisfy our selfish desires, but he prospers us that we can have more to give. It is not giving for our sake, but giving so that we might have a means of giving to others. He says, "And God is able to make all grace abound toward you; that ye, always having all sufficiency in all things, may abound to every good work" (2 Cor. 9:8). So that we will be "enriched in every thing to all bountifulness" (2 Cor. 9:11).

He is saying that God is going to bless you according to his power and ability so that you will have more to give. Now that again is contrary to reason. It doesn't stand to reason that the more you give the more you will have to give. Reason says the more that you save the more you will have to give. That is the way it seems. But God has a way of multiplying what we have. If we will respond to God and to people, then God blesses what we give so that we have more to give. It's like the widow's pot of oil (1 Kings 17:16). The more we give, the more we have. We do not know God's bounty until we begin to use it.

One of my men said to me recently as we were talking about stewardship, "I am never going to tithe again." I nearly had a heart attack. Then he explained, "Since we started the building program (at our church) and I started giving above my tithe to it, I have been blessed in more ways than I can number." He said, "We used to scrimp and save to meet the bills at the end of the month. Now when the end of the month comes, we have paid all of our bills and there is still something left over." I didn't ask for the testimony. I didn't try to drag that out of him. I didn't tell him what to say. He shared it on his own. He was saying that the more he gave the more he had to give. I have seen it work not only in individual lives, but also in my church.

A few years ago we were struggling along with our budget and there came a challenge that we ought to give above and beyond it. We agreed that everything that was given above and beyond our budget would go to missions, evangelism, and outreach. We would give it away. And that year we oversubscribed our budget by $49,000 and we over-gave it by $60,000. It seemed as though the more we gave away, the more we had to give. You can call that a coincidence if you want to. I believe it is more than a coincidence. I believe it is a principle of life. The more you give, the more God gives you to give. God knows there are needs everywhere and he wants you to be a channel of blessing.

We are tempted quite often to say of wealthy people, "If I just had what they have, I would give more." That is not the way it works. They don't give because they have. The reverse is more likely true. They have because they give. You need to take the initiative. You need to prime the pump. You need to get the resources flowing.

Some of you remember the old days when people had pumps that had to be primed in order to get water. There was an abundance of water in the well below and there was a pump. But after the pump sat for awhile, the leather gasket on the plunger would get dry and hard. It wouldn't form a suction to draw the water. So you had to pour some water down in the pump to get that leather washer wet. Then it would swell and form a suction and draw the water up. You had to prime it if you wanted water.

That is what God is saying in this passage of Scripture. You need to prime the pump. You need to get the water flowing. You will discover that God's well has a limitless resource to bless and satisfy your needs.

I am persuaded that these three principles are true-to-life. The way, the surest way, to have is to share. Give according to God's ability, not your own, and if you will do this your life will be blessed. I want to challenge you to take God at his word. If you don't believe me, search it out. See if what I said is true. And then by faith, act on it. Do something about it. God will bless you and you will be amazed at what God will do.

12
Enduring—How to Avoid a Spiritual Relapse

Mark Twain, in his book *Tom Sawyer*, tells about the time Tom got the measles:

During two long weeks Tom lay a prisoner, dead to the world and its happenings. He was very ill; he was interested in nothing. When he got upon his feet at last and moved feebly downtown, a melancholy change had come over everything and every creature. There had been a revival, and everybody had 'got religion,' not only the adults, but even the boys and girls. Tom went about, hoping against hope for the sight of one blessed sinful face, but disappointment crossed him everywhere. He found Joe Harper studying a Testament, and turned sadly away from the depressing spectacle. He sought Ben Rogers, and found him visiting the poor with a basket of tracts. He hunted up Jim Hollis, who called his attention to the precious blessing of his late measles as a warning. Every boy he encountered added another ton to his depression; and when, in desperation, he flew for refuge at last to the bosom of Huckleberry Finn and was received with a scriptural quotation, his heart broke and he crept home and to bed realizing that he alone of all the town was lost, forever and forever.

The next day the doctors were back; Tom had re-lapsed. The three weeks he spent on his back this time seemed an entire age. When he got abroad at last he was hardly grateful that he had been spared, remembering how lonely was his estate, how companionless and for-lorn he was. He drifted listlessly down the street and found Jim Hollis acting as judge in a juvenile court that was trying a cat for murder, in the presence of her victim, a bird. He found Joe Harper and Huck Finn up an alley eating a stolen melon.

Then the author interjects the thought, "Poor lads! They . . . like Tom . . . had suffered a relapse."

People can suffer a spiritual relapse. It is possible to receive Christ as Savior, experience the thrill and joy of salvation, and then relapse back into the old way of life. It is the purpose of this chapter to help you avoid a spiritual relapse. There are five things that will help.

Understand What Happened to You When You Became a Christian

Basically, three things took place when you were saved.

First, you were given a new position, a new standing, with God. The Bible calls it being justified (Rom. 5:1). The word *"justified"* is a legal term which means "I become before God 'just-as-if-I'd' never sinned." When you believed in Christ, your sins were forgiven and forgotten by God. He saw you and accepted you just as if you had never sinned.

Second, you were given a new potential, a new power,

from Christ. When you accepted Christ, his Spirit (the Holy Spirit), came to live inside you to empower you, strengthen you, and enable you to live the Christian life. There is now in you the power to become all God wants you to be.

Third, you were given a new purpose, a new desire, for life. The magnificent obsession of your life now is to do the will of God. Whereas you once lived only to do your own will, your purpose has changed and God's will is preeminent.

Remember this—temptation and difficulties are still very real. There will be hardships, trials, and failures. Don't be discouraged. Just remember that you have a new position, a new potential, and a new purpose. Seek to understand them better.

Rely on the Holy Spirit to Help You

As I have already said, the moment you receive Christ as your Savior, the Holy Spirit of God comes to live inside you (1 Cor. 6:19–20). It is his power that will enable you to live a victorious Christian life. God never intended that you live by your own strength. That's why he sent the Holy Spirit.

Three verses of Scripture will help clarify our need of the Holy Spirit. The first reads, "Whether therefore ye eat, or drink, or whatsoever ye do, do all to the glory of God" (1 Cor. 10:31).

The second says, "For all have sinned, and come short of the glory of God" (Rom. 3:23).

The third is, "To whom God would make known what

is the riches of the glory of this mystery among the Gentiles; which is Christ in you, the hope of glory" (Col. 1:27).

The first verse tells us that the purpose of life is the glory of God. This is the purpose of both creation and redemption. The second verse tells us that the hindrance to life is sin. The final verse tells us that the hope of life is Christ in us. To live life as it should be lived, we must draw upon God's power. By daily prayer and Bible study we can draw continually upon His power.

The Holy Spirit is the difference in victory and failure in Christian living. The difference in Peter, when he denied Christ and when he defied the court order to stop preaching, was the Holy Spirit. The Holy Spirit can be that difference in your life also.

Develop a Strong Devotional Life

Learning how to pray and how to study the Bible are imperatives. Prayer is as essential to our spiritual life as breathing is to our physical life. The Bible is the spiritual food by which we grow (1 Pet. 2:2).

The Bible is a closed book and prayer is a lost art to many Christians today. Yet both of them are essential for a vital relationship with God. A good devotional life demands discipline. Most of us flounder on indecisiveness. We know we need a devotional life, but never say to ourselves, "OK, tomorrow morning at 6:00 A.M. I begin." It takes that kind of determination to do it. Set yourself a time and place and begin. (For specific suggestions see chapter 3, Six Ways to Study the Bible.)

Remember this—Satan will do all he can to keep you
from having a strong devotional life. If he can win here,
he wins the victory and you will live a defeated life.
Brace up! Discipline yourself. Pray and read God's Word
daily and you will avoid a spiritual relapse.

Live by Faith and Not by Feelings

Faith means taking God at his word. But what is God's
Word? It is the Bible. If I live by faith, it means that I
accept what God has said in the Bible as true and I rest in
confidence on it. This is the only grounds for confidence
in the Christian life. My feelings come and go. They
depend on the weather, or the last phone call I received,
or whether or not my wife burned the toast at breakfast.
Thank goodness, my relationship to God is based on a
surer foundation.

Satan will raise many doubts in your mind. When they
come, only reliance on God's Word will sustain you. For
example, Satan will ask you, "How do you know you are
really saved?" When that doubt arises, you should answer it with Romans 10:13, "For whosoever shall call
upon the name of the Lord shall be saved." In this verse
God has given you a promise and a condition. His promise is to save. The condition is that you must call on him
in prayer. Since you have met the condition by calling on
God to save you, the responsibility is his to do it. If God
is trustworthy, you have been saved. God cannot lie
(Titus 1:2), so thank him for what he has done and rest in
that confidence.

Again, Satan will ask you "How do you know your sins

are forgiven?" You should answer him with, "If we confess our sins, he is faithful and just to forgive us our sins,
and to cleanse us from all unrighteousness" (1 John 1:9).
Again, God gives us a promise and a condtion in this
verse. The promise is for forgiveness and cleansing of all
our sins. The condition is "if we confess." Have you done
that? If so, you have met God's condition and he is honor
bound to keep his word. He is "faithful and just." He will
do it. Thank him for forgiving you and do not fret over it.

If you live by *your* feelings, your life will be filled with
frustrations and anxiety. If you live by faith, you can have
peace and confidence and assurance.

Find a Place of Service and Go to Work for God

As believers, we are to abound in the word of the Lord
(1 Cor. 15:58). This means that we are to witness and
serve, not just go to church. The first thing you should
do is tell your family and friends what Christ has done for
you. Tell them how your life used to be, how you came to
faith, and what a difference Christ has made in your life.
Encourage them to accept Christ also.

I have an alcoholic friend who has been dry for several
years. Occasionally, when he feels a compulsion to go
back into the old life and get drunk, he goes to the city
jail and asks to talk to prisoners. He tells them how he
used to be and how much better his new life is. He said,
"I ensure my own sobriety by telling others." We do the
same thing. A relapse can be serious. Avoid it at all costs.
If you will follow these five guides, you will grow stronger
and healthier and happier in your new life.